ULTIMATE RANDOM TRIVIA BOOK

Publications International, Ltd.

CONTENTS

A LITTLE OF THIS, A LITTLE OF THAT, PLUS A LOT OF OTHER THINGS

Prepare yourself. From the astounding to the merely bemusing, this collection is packed with all kinds of trivia, history, science, canny speculation, and debunkery. Each chapter is organized around a loose theme—from music to pessimism to the concept of time—and every article pushes that theme in a new direction. You'll find sports and games explored from every angle, the history behind pivotal and peculiar inventions (how did we get kitty litter anyway?), a smattering of espionage and military history, and all kinds of other random stuff. Each chapter ends with 10 multiple choice trivia questions. You're sure to come away with a little more knowledge—about a whole lot of things.

ALL I GOT WAS THIS LOUSY T-SHIRT

Tourism works like this: You go to a place, and the people in charge of the place take all your money. And you're okay with that. It's a peculiar setup, but it's part of a venerable tradition with roots that trace back to the ancient world. Having gone there gives you bragging rights: you'll be able to say you were there before they (Hittites, Canadians, whatever) ruined the scenery. Losing it all in Vegas, getting fleeced outside St. Peter's, getting overcharged for a delousing in Lima—it beats a stupid t-shirt.

WHAT WAS TRAVEL LIKE IN ANCIENT TIMES?

My Folks Went to Athens and All I Got Was This Lousy Peplos

What did the very earliest tourists—if there were any at all—enjoy? Cuddly saber-toothed kittens at the petting zoo? Tar pit paddle boat rides? Well, that was prehistory, and tourism wasn't yet an industry, but with the passing of many centuries, city-states and empires became sophisticated enough that tourism was feasible. Visitors couldn't enjoy Six Flags over Carthage, but that's only because it hadn't been invented. There were other places to go and things to see, but travel beyond one's own borders was nevertheless a risky proposition.

By the first millennium BC, Near Eastern empires had developed waterways, roads, lodging, and systems of commerce sufficient to encourage tourism. Even better, there was a mass of potential tourists to make added investment in infrastructure worthwhile. Then with the rise of the Persian Empire in mid-millennium (around 500 BC), two additional key elements—peace and effective government—made tourism not just possible but relatively pleasant.

The earliest tourist destinations evident in the Western historical record are Babylon (present-day Iraq) and Egypt. Both destinations had neat things to see: the Hanging Gardens, pyramids, temples, festivals, and street markets. The ancient world also had museums, lighthouses, religious celebrations, and a lively system of commerce to lure well-heeled visitors.

Going Greek

When Greece caught the attention of curious travelers around 500 BC, visitors favored the safer sea route rather than brave the wilds of Asia Minor (modern Turkey). At about the same time, the Levantine ports of what are now Syria, Lebanon, and Israel flourished. In the 400s BC, Greeks wrote travel guides that evaluated locations and facilities—a little like *Lonely Planet*, but at that time the known limits of the planet were much smaller.

Greek and Levantine destinations attracted visitors, but these tourists still had to remain on guard. In those days, people carried cash (no credit cards, right?), which attracted the attention of swindlers, pickpockets, and cutthroats. Seas around favored ports were controlled well enough to allow local and regional commerce to thrive, but a ship full of people wearing the ancient equivalent of Bermuda shorts was easy prey for pirates. Until things became safer and easier, tourism couldn't grow.

Roamin' Romans

With its seafaring rival Carthage put out of the way by 202 BC, Republican Rome began its rise to undisputed dominance of the Mediterranean Sea. By the time Rome had a bona fide empire (about 27 BC), well-laid Roman roads encircled *Mare Nostrum* ("our sea"), with inns spaced just a day's travel apart. Armed patrols ensured the security of land routes. The Roman fleet aggressively hunted down pirates, making sea travel safer than ever before. Roman maps told travelers where they might go; chroniclers offered details about the sites.

Many would-be travelers had the hardy soul that was required, but then as today, serious travel was for the affluent. Most Romans were too poor to enjoy the diversions of new places. And even for those who could afford visits to Athens, Judea, and Egypt, the land route meant overpriced food of unpredictable quality and uncomfortable lodging.

The Mediterranean's sea lanes may have been swept of pirates, but nothing could be done about storms and other nautical hazards. Mindful of this risk, Romans struck bargains with the gods before travel, promising to do this or that in return for a safe voyage. Of course, even the most attentive Roman gods couldn't guarantee a *pleasant* trip.

Fun and Games for Grownups

So what was there to see and do around *Mare Nostrum?* For the pleasures of gluttony and sin, one might try the western Italian coast. Although Sparta was some 300 years into decline by AD 1, travelers were drawn there by the echoes of its martial past and by the quaint Spartan notion of equality between the sexes.

Athens had reached its peak around the fifth century BC, and was in decline by the first century AD, but swarmed with visitors drawn by the city's architecture and sculpture. Egypt's pyramids remained an attraction, and Alexandria still had a fabulous library. Then there was *Novum Ilium* (New Troy), also known as Troy IX, as the site had been destroyed or abandoned, and subsequently rebuilt, many times over the centuries. In 85 BC, the Romans put it back together as a living memorial to their supposed Trojan heritage, with enough Greek and Persian touches tacked on to further intrigue travelers.

Other Mediterranean destinations and diversions included zoos, freak shows, prostitutes, exotic foods—and above all, bragging rights for having undertaken a pleasure trip in the first place. The ancient traveler was considered nothing if not cosmopolitan.

Eternal Rome

Because "Rome" signified a still-vast empire by the first century AD, the city not only provided a class of tourists who traveled from the city, but hosted countless citizens who came to Rome from the empire's farther reaches. These visitors were inevitably impressed, and not a little intimidated, by the city's sprawl, grime, and confusion.

More than a million people lived in Rome, and the effect of the city upon visitors from quieter realms must have been breathtaking—and not always in a pleasant way. Still, any provincial who returned from *Roma Eterna* was hailed back home as a sophisticate, just as a Roman who could speak gracefully about the ancient route of the Greek poet Homer enjoyed an elevated social status.

As Rome declined, so did tourism, but pleasure travel never died out completely. Although today's Mediterranean tour guides, bus drivers, trinket sellers, and desk clerks may not realize it, they are practitioners of a popular art that is ancient and perhaps even noble.

ARE THE PYRAMIDS OF EGYPT THE OLDEST MONUMENTS IN THE WORLD?

Ask most people what they consider the oldest, most venerable and magnificent architecture in the world, and the pyramids are sure to be a common answer. Magnificent they are, but they are not the oldest.

The Pyramids of Giza are the most famous monuments of ancient Egypt and the only structures remaining of the original Seven Wonders of the Ancient World. Originally about 480 feet high, they are also the largest stone structures constructed by humans. But there are older monuments.

What's older than the pyramids? That glory goes to the prehistoric temples of Malta—a small island south of Sicily. The temples date from 4000 to 2500 BC. At approximately 6,000 years old, they are a thousand years older than the pyramids. Not much is known about the people who built these magnificent structures, but they were likely farmers who constructed the temples as public places of worship.

Because the Maltese temples were covered with soil from early times and not discovered until the 19th century, these megalithic structures have been well preserved. Extensive archaeological and restorative work was carried out in the early 20th century by European and Maltese archaeologists to further ensure the temples' longevity. The major temple complexes are now designated as UNESCO World Heritage Sites.

Which pyramid is the oldest? That would be the Step Pyramid at Saqqara. It was built during the third dynasty of Egypt's Old Kingdom to protect the body of King Djoser, who died around 2649 BC. It was this architectural feat that propelled the construction of the gigantic stone pyramids of ancient Egypt on a rocky desert plateau close to the Nile. These pyramids, known as the Great Pyramids, were built around 2493 BC. The largest structure served as the tomb for Pharaoh Khufu.

WHY ARE THERE GIANT STONE HEADS ON EASTER ISLAND?

A Dutch ship landed on a small island 2,300 miles from the coast of South America on Easter Sunday, 1722. They found the island was inhabited. They also found a strange collection of almost 900 enormous stone heads, or *moai*. The image of those faces haunts visitors to this day.

Ancestors at the End of the Land

Easter Island legend tells of the great Chief Hotu Matu'a, the Great Parent, striking out from Polynesia in a canoe, taking his family on a voyage across the trackless ocean in search of a new home. He made landfall on Te-Pito-te-Henua, the End of the Land, sometime between AD 400 and 700. Finding the island suitable for habitation, his descendants spread out to cover much of the island, living off the natural bounty of the land and sea. With their survival assured, they built *ahu*—ceremonial sites featuring a large stone mound—and on them erected moai, which were representations of notable chieftains who led the island over the centuries. The moai weren't literal depictions of their ancestors, but rather embodied their spirit, and conferred blessings and protection on the islanders.

The construction of these moai was quite a project. A hereditary class of sculptors oversaw the main quarry, located near one of the volcanic mountains on the island. Groups of people would request a moai for their local ahu, and the sculptors would go to work, their efforts supported by gifts of food and other goods. Over time, they created 887 of the stone moai, averaging just over 13 feet tall and weighing around 14 tons, but ranging from one extreme of just under four feet tall to a behemoth that towered 71 feet. The moai were then transported across the island by a mechanism that still remains in doubt, but that may have involved rolling them on the trunks of palm trees felled for that purpose—a technique that was to have terrible repercussions for the islanders.

When Europeans first made landfall on Easter Island, they found an island full of standing moai. Half a century later, James Cook reported that many of the statues had been toppled, and by the 1830s none were left standing. What's more, the statues hadn't just been knocked over; many of them had boulders placed at strategic locations, with the intention of decapitating the moai when they were pulled down. What happened?

A Culture on the Brink

It turns out the original Dutch explorers had encountered a culture on the rebound. At the time of their arrival, they found two or three thousand people living on the island, but some estimates put the population as high as fifteen thousand only a century before. The story of the islanders' decline is one in which many authors find a cautionary tale: the people simply consumed natural resources to the point where their land could no longer support them.

For a millennium, the islanders simply took whatever they needed: they fished, collected bird eggs, and chopped down trees to pursue their obsession with building moai. By the 1600s, life had changed: the last forests on the island had disappeared, and the islanders' traditional foodstuffs disappeared from the archaeological record. Local tradition tells of a time of famine and even rumored cannibalism, and it is from this dark time that island history reveals the appearance of the spear. Tellingly, the Polynesian words for "wood" begin to take on a connotation of wealth, a semantic meaning found nowhere else that shares the language. Perhaps worst of all, with their forests gone, the islanders had no material to make the canoes that would have allowed them to leave their island in search of new resources. They were trapped, and they turned on one another.

The Europeans found an impoverished society that had just emerged from this time of terror. The respite was short-lived, however. The arrival of the foreigners seems to have come at a critical moment in the history of Easter Island. Either coincidentally or spurred on by the strangers, a warrior class seized power across the island, and different groups vied for power. Villages were burned, their resources taken by the victors, and the defeated left to starve. The warfare also led to the toppling of an enemy's moai—whether to capture their mana or simply prevent it from being used against the opposing faction. In the end, none of the moai remained standing.

Downfall and Rebound

The troubles of the island weren't limited to self-inflicted chaos. The arrival of the white man also introduced smallpox and syphilis; the islanders, with little immunity to the diseases, fared no better than native populations elsewhere. As if that weren't enough, other ships arrived, collecting slaves for work in South America. Internal fighting and external pressure combined to reduce the number of islanders to little more than a hundred by 1877—the last survivors of a people who once enjoyed a tropical paradise. Easter Island was annexed by Chile in 1888. As of 2012, the island's population was approaching 6,000. Projects are underway to raise the fallen moai. As of today, approximately 50 have been returned to their former glory.

IS TIMBUKTU AN ACTUAL PLACE?

The city of Timbuktu lives in the English vocabulary as a mythical place remembered for its unique, lyrical name. Yes, it exists. The real Timbuktu is a small city in northwestern Africa. It is located in central Mali about 500 miles from the Atlantic coast on the Niger River. Its roughly 30,000 inhabitants are mostly of Tuareg, Songhai, Fulani, or Moorish heritage.

The Name

The Tuaregs, a nomadic people of the Sahara region, founded Timbuktu sometime around AD 1000. The story goes that a well-respected lady named Buktu lived near a well ("tin" in Tuareg). Nomads who needed to leave things behind entrusted them to Buktu and said they had left their possessions at "Tin Buktu." Ms. Buktu is long gone, but her name has endured. Even today, there is a well said to be that of Buktu herself.

The Place

Timbuktu began as an encampment and grew into a town, becoming an important stop on the trans-Saharan trade route. Salt mined from the Sahara went south and west; slaves and gold went north toward the Mediterranean. Even though Timbuktu changed hands among African empires, it developed into a prestigious Islamic cultural and religious center.

In its peak era beginning in about 1330, Timbuktu had 100,000 residents, including 25,000 students. The prized turban of a Timbuktu scholar proclaimed its wearer to be a devout Muslim steeped in Islamic learning. In order to receive the lowest of four degrees conferred in Timbuktu, the student had to memorize the entire Koran. Learned scholars coming to Timbuktu from afar required extra teaching to bring their knowledge up to local standards. In terms of prestige, it might be fair to call Timbuktu the Oxford of the medieval Islamic world.

The golden era ended in 1591, when Moroccans conquered the Songhai Empire. The Moroccan conquest didn't kill Timbuktu, but the city was mortally wounded as trade routes shifted after the year 1600. Carrying goods across the sea became safer and faster than hauling everything across the Sahara. The city became something of a backwater, yet remained an important destination for dedicated students seeking immersion in Islam.

By the 1800s, Timbuktu was only known as a legend to Europeans. A French exploration society offered a bounty to anyone who visited and returned to describe it. One Frenchman named René-Auguste Caillé finally returned with an account of the city. His report would have made a lousy tourist brochure, as he found only a collection of mud huts threatened by the rising sands of the Sahara. The only remarkable aspects of Timbuktu, Caillé said, were its centers of Islamic learning.

In 1960, Mali achieved independence. At that time Timbuktu hadn't changed much since Caillé's visit. But the city's prominence has risen in recent years. Today it is called "The Mecca of Africa" for the prestigious courses offered at the city's Sankore Mosque. Refusing to be forgotten again, the city has even managed to keep the Sahara's drifting sands at bay.

WHY WAS THE TAJ MAHAL BUILT?

The Mughal Empire occupied India from the mid-1500s to the early 1800s. At the height of its success, this imperial power controlled most of the Indian subcontinent and much of what is now Afghanistan, containing a population of around 150 million people. During this era, a young prince named Khurram took the throne in 1628, succeeding his father. Six years prior, after a military victory, Khurram was given the title *Shah Jahan* by his emperor father.

Now, with much of the subcontinent at his feet, the title was apt: Shah Jahan is Persian for "King of the World." (17th-century emperors were nothing if not modest.)

When Khurram Met Arjumand

Being shah had a lot of fringe benefits—banquets, treasures, and multiple wives, among other things. Shah Jahan did have several wives, but one woman stood out from the rest. When he was age 15, he was betrothed to 14-year-old Arjumand Banu Begam. Her beauty and compassion knocked the emperor-to-be off his feet; five years later, they were married. The bride took the title of *Mumtaz Mahal*, which means, according to various translations, "Chosen One of the Palace," "Exalted One of the Palace," or "Beloved Ornament of the Palace." You get the point.

Court historians have recorded the couple's close friendship, companionship, and intimate relationship. The couple traveled extensively together, Mumtaz often accompanying her husband on his military jaunts. But tragedy struck in 1631, when on one of these trips, Mumtaz died giving birth to what would have been their 14th child.

Breaking Ground

Devastated, Shah Jahan began work that year on what would become the Taj Mahal, a palatial monument to his dead wife. While there were surely many hands on deck for the planning of the Taj, the architect who is most often credited is Ustad Ahmad Lahori. The project took until 1648 to complete and enlisted the labor of 20,000 workers and 1,000 elephants.

The structure and surrounding grounds cover 42 acres. The following are the basic parts of Mumtaz's giant mausoleum.

The Gardens: To get to the structural parts of the Taj Mahal, one must cross the enormous gardens surrounding it. Following classic Persian garden design, the grounds to the south of the buildings are made up of four sections divided by marble canals (reflecting pools) with adjacent pathways. The gardens stretch from the main gateway to the foot of the Taj.

The Main Gateway: Made of red sandstone and standing approximately 100 feet high and 150 feet wide, the main gateway is composed of a central arch with towers attached to each of its corners. The walls are richly adorned with calligraphy and floral arabesques inlaid with gemstones.

The Tomb: Unlike most Mughal mausoleums, Mumtaz's tomb is placed at the north end of the Taj Mahal, above the river and in between the mosque and the guesthouse. The tomb is entirely sheathed in white marble with an exterior dome that is almost 250 feet above ground level. The effect is impressive. Depending on the light at various times of the day, the tomb can appear pink, white, or brilliant gold.

The Mosque and the Jawab: On either side of the great tomb lie two smaller buildings. One is a mosque, and the other is called the *jawab*, or "answer." The mosque was used, of course, as a place of worship; the jawab was often used as a guesthouse. Both buildings are made of red sandstone so as not to take away too much from the grandeur of the tomb. The shah's monument to the love of his life still stands, more than 360 years later.

HOW DID CENTRAL PARK GET THERE?

A stroll through New York City's Central Park might lead you to believe that it is the one remaining slice of nature amid the towering skyscrapers of steel and glass that flank it. But this urban park is almost entirely human-made. And even though Manhattan's northern half was laid out in the early 19th century, the park was not part of the Commissioners' Plan of 1811.

Between 1821 and 1855, the population of New York nearly quadrupled. This growth convinced city planners that a large, open-air space was required. Initial plans mimicked the large public grounds of London and Paris, but it was eventually decided that the space should evoke feelings of nature—complete with running water, dense wooded areas, and even rolling hills.

The original park layout included the area stretching from 59th to 106th streets and also included land between 5th and 8th avenues. The land cost about $5 million. This part of Manhattan featured an irregular terrain of swamps and bluffs and included rocky outcrops left from the last Ice Age 10,000 years earlier; it was deemed unsuitable for private development but was ideal for creating the park that leaders envisioned. However, the area was not uninhabited. It was home to about 1,600 poor residents, most of them Irish and German immigrants—though there was a thriving African American community there as well. Ultimately, these groups were resettled, and the park's boundaries were extended to 110th street.

Just Wild Enough

In the 1850s, the state of New York appointed a Central Park Commission to oversee the development of the park. A landscape design contest was held in 1857, and writer and landscape architect Frederick Law Olmsted and architect Calvert Vaux won with their "Greensward Plan." Olmsted and Vaux envisioned a park that would include "separate circulation systems" for its assorted users, including pedestrians and horseback riders. To accommodate crosstown traffic while still maintaining the sense of a continuous single park, the roads that traversed Central Park from East to West were sunken and screened with planted shrub belts. Likewise, the Greensward Plan called for three dozen bridges, all designed by Vaux, with no two alike. These included simple granite bridges as well as ornate neogothic conceptions made of cast iron. The southern portion of the park was designed to include the mall walk to Bethesda Terrace and Bethesda Fountain, which provided a view of the lake and woodland to the north.

Central Park was one of the largest public works projects in New York during the 19th century, with some 20,000 workers on hand to reshape the topography of nearly 850 acres. Massive amounts of gunpowder (more, in fact, than was used in the Battle of Gettysburg) were used to blast the rocky ridges, and nearly three million cubic yards of soil were moved. At the same time, some 270,000 trees and shrubs were planted to replicate the feeling of nature.

Despite the massive scale of work involved, the park first opened for public use in 1858; by 1865, it was receiving more than seven million visitors a year. Strict rules on group picnics and certain activities kept some New York residents away, but by the 1880s, the park was as welcoming to the working class as it was to the wealthy.

Over time, the park welcomed a number of additions, including the famous Carousel and Zoo, and activities such as tennis and bike riding became part of the landscape. Today, Central Park plays host to concerts, Shakespeare plays, swimming, and ice-skating. It also features a welcoming bird sanctuary for watchers and their feathered friends alike and is a pleasant urban retreat for millions of New Yorkers.

WHAT'S THE MOST CROWDED PLACE ON EARTH?

No, it's not Disneyland on the first day of summer vacation. And it's not the Mall of America on the morning after Thanksgiving either. While those places are definitely hectic at certain times, there is a section of Hong Kong that has them both beat 365 days a year.

Packed Like Sardines

It's called Mong Kok, which translates to "flourishing/busy corner." The name is apt because, according to *Guinness World Records*, Mong Kok is the most densely populated place on the planet. About 200,000 people reside in Mong Kok, an area just slightly larger than half a square mile. That's about 70 square feet per person. Add in the buildings and you've got a district in which it is physically impossible for everyone to be outside at the same time.

Mong Kok's bustling Golden Mile—a popular stretch of shops, restaurants, and theaters—compounds the crowding issue: a half-million or so tourists routinely jostle for position in the streets. Residents told *The New York Times* that the streets are often completely full, with every inch of pavement covered.

Going Up, Up, Up

How is it possible to squeeze so many people into such a small area? You build up. Mong Kok is home to an array of high-rise apartment buildings. Families who live in these apartments sometimes rent out rooms to other families. There might be ten or more people in a single apartment—they sleep in two or three rooms and share a small kitchen and a single bathroom. The apartments are so small that people sleep in bunk beds that are three or four tiers high, and they keep their belongings in chests and baskets that are suspended from the ceiling. Remember that the next time you're elbowing your way through a crowded store on Black Friday, trying to secure the season's must-have toy. When you return home and sit at the table for dinner, at least there won't be two other families smiling back at you.

HOW DID VEGAS BECOME VEGAS?

There's really no place in the world like Las Vegas. It's a world-renowned mecca for gaming, entertainment, and shopping. Once a mobster paradise, the city now bills itself as the Entertainment Capital of the World, and it's still a place where one can get into trouble without actually getting into *trouble*.

Before all the lights and splendor, however, Las Vegas wasn't much of anything. It began as a 19th-century pioneer trail outpost where desert-weary California-bound settlers drew fresh water from the artesian wells in the surrounding Las Vegas Valley.

No Gambling? No Dice!

In 1905, Las Vegas became a railroad town (incorporated as the City of Las Vegas in 1911) with service facilities, supply stores, and saloons. But Vegas's growth was stunted for the next two decades when in 1909, the Nevada legislature killed the best thing the town had going for it: legalized gambling.

The Appeal of the Gambling Repeal

In 1931, Nevada repealed the ban on gambling, ostensibly to raise tax money to fund its school system but also to undermine the state's thriving illegal gambling industry. Soon downtown Las Vegas became host to a slew of roughneck casinos sporting a few slot machines, gaming tables, and—in some cases—sawdust floors.

That same year, construction began on the Hoover Dam 34 miles south of Las Vegas, bringing an unprecedented influx of workers and tourists to southern Nevada. But with nothing to do in nearby Boulder City (the town built by the federal government for dam workers where alcohol, gaming, and fun remained illegal), workers and tourists alike streamed north along Highway 91, heading to Vegas to find entertainment.

The Strip Is Born

One man, Thomas Hull (owner of the El Rancho motel chain), noticed the busy traffic—particularly the heavy flow of Vegas-bound travelers from Los Angeles. Seeking to attract their business, Hull opened the El Rancho Vegas in April 1941 on a stretch of Highway 91 just south of Vegas city limits. This area eventually morphed into the famous Las Vegas Strip.

The El Rancho wasn't your typical Vegas gaming joint. The sprawling Spanish mission-style complex featured a main casino building surrounded by such amenities as 65 guest cottages, a swimming pool, a nightclub, a steakhouse, retail shopping, and recreation areas. It had a casual "boots and jeans" ambience that placed an emphasis on comfort and pleasure. The El Rancho brought gambling and vacationing together in Vegas's first casino resort and became the model for future casinos.

Observing the success of the El Rancho, movie theater mogul R. E. Griffith emulated Hull's model and added a new dimension. In October 1942, Griffith opened the Hotel Last Frontier on the site of the old Pair-O-Dice nightclub near the El Rancho. Aiming to trump the El Rancho, Griffith designed the Last Frontier around an Old West theme, featuring frontier-style decor, genuine historical artifacts, and costumed employees. Griffith thus introduced the fantasy theme concept to Vegas. Consequently, the stage was set for the notorious Benjamin "Bugsy" Siegel, who in 1946, with the opening of the Mafiabankrolled Flamingo down the road from the Last Frontier, elevated Hull's and Griffith's prototypes to new heights. Siegel spared no expense in creating an ultra-glitzy, ultra-glamorous "carpet joint" (to use his words) designed to lure the wealthy Hollywood set. His loose spending of mob money—combined with his girlfriend's penchant for skimming Flamingo cash—eventually cost Siegel his life. But Siegel established the trend of over-the-top luxury casino resorts that define Vegas today, and he brought an alluring mob mystique to Vegas that put the city on the map for good.

WHO PICKED THE SEVEN WONDERS ANYWAY?

Even the Ancients Liked Making Lists

Humans have always loved their lists—to-do, to-avoid, best-of, grocery, bucket, top ten, payback—so it makes sense that we would obsessively list cool stuff to see. There is a "wonder list" for every kind of wonder imaginable. The original and most famous list is the Seven Wonders of the Ancient World, or "Six You'll Have to Take Our Word for, Plus One You Can Actually See."

One of the earliest references to "wonders" is in the writings of Greek historian Herodotus from the fifth century BC. Herodotus wrote extensively about some of the impressive wonders he had seen and heard about. However, the concept of the Seven Wonders didn't really catch on until the second century BC. For the next fifteen hundred or so years, six of the seven were a sure lock, often showing up on various compiled lists, with the seventh spot being a rotating roster of hopefuls. By the time the list solidified and became the accepted seven of today (some time around the Renaissance), the Lighthouse of Alexandria had taken up the seventh spot.

No single person actually got to choose the seven; it was more of a generally accepted concept based on the frequency with which certain wonders landed on different lists. Furthermore, by the time the Middle Ages had rolled around, most of the wonders could not be seen in their full glory because of damage, erosion, or destruction, so the selections were based primarily on reputation. For example, that lighthouse? A series of medieval earthquakes took their toll, and by 1480, its few remaining foundation stones were being carted away to build the Citadel of Qaitbay.

And so . . . the Seven Wonders of the Ancient World were the Pyramids of Giza in Egypt, the Hanging Gardens of Babylon in Iraq, the Statue of Zeus at Olympia in Greece, the Mausoleum of Maussollos at Halicarnassus in Turkey, the Colossus of Rhodes, the Temple of Artemis at Ephesus, and the Lighthouse of Alexandria in Egypt.

The Pyramids of Giza are the Energizer Bunny of the seven wonders. They were by far the oldest when the lists began, and they are the only wonder still standing today. On the other hand, some of the other wonders had relatively short lifespans. The Colossus of Rhodes was big in size (about 107 feet high) but not very big on longevity—the statue stood for a mere 54 years. However, it was impressive enough to stay in the minds of list-makers. The Temple of Artemis was rebuilt three times but was gone by AD 401. Of the seven, the Hanging Gardens of Babylon is the only wonder whose actual location has never been established.

In 2001, the New 7 Wonders Foundation was established by a Swiss businessman. The foundation's intention was to create an updated list of the seven wonders of the world based on an online vote. (Notably, users could vote more than once.) In 2007, the wonders chosen were Chichén Itzá in Mexico, Christ the Redeemer in Brazil, the Colosseum in Rome, the Great Wall of China, Machu Picchu in Peru, Petra in Jordan, and the Taj Mahal in India. The Pyramids of Giza were subsequently awarded honorary finalist status after Egypt complained that these great historical structures shouldn't have to compete against such young whippersnappers.

So make your own lists, and bury them in a time capsule. Maybe one day that cool treehouse you built with your dad will finally get its due.

1. What city is the Colosseum located in?
a. Carthage
b. Rome
c. London
d. Venice

2. The country of Peru is famous for this ancient site.
a. Chicxulub
b. Stonehenge
c. Chichén Itzá
d. Machu Picchu

3. The Golden Gate Bridge connects San Francisco with:
a. Marin County
b. Oakland
c. Alcatraz Island
d. Los Angeles

4. The Sydney Opera House can be found here:
a. Sydney, Italy
b. Sydney, Mexico
c. Sydney, South Africa
d. Sydney, Australia

5. Where is Hadrian's Wall?
a. United Kingdom
b. Denmark
c. Portugal
d. Ireland

6. Hagia Sophia is one of Turkey's most famous buildings. It is located in this city.
a. Cairo
b. Ankara
c. Istanbul
d. Athens

7. What's the biggest city in North America, by population?
a. Toronto
b. Mexico City
c. Los Angeles
d. Havana

8. The Great Pyramid of Giza is located in Egypt, a country found in:
a. Europe
b. South America
c. Africa
d. Australia

9. In what city can you find the Liberty Bell?
a. Boston
b. Philadelphia
c. New York City
d. Baltimore

10. In what city can you find Big Ben?
a. London
b. Boston
c. Vancouver
d. Melbourne

1.
b. Rome

2.
d. Machu Picchu

3.
a. Marin County

4.
d. Sydney, Australia

5.
a. United Kingdom

6.
c. Istanbul

7.
b. Mexico City

8.
c. Africa

9.
b. Philadelphia

10.
a. London

INVENTIONS

WELL, IT DIDN'T MAKE ITSELF

People are always inventing things, useful or otherwise. It's a compulsion, really. We may complain about artificial environments, threaten to go back to nature, sell off the Bunsen burners—but then the tinkering starts: "I wonder how it would perform if we vulcanized it,*" or "I just want to improve the signal a bit—got this idea for using* fiber optics.*" And then no one sees us at holiday parties because we're holed up in the garage just tinkering a bit with some* graphene supercapacitors. *All because we can't stop inventing new things.*

WHERE DID THE VENDING MACHINE COME FROM?

Vending machines seem to be distinctly modern contraptions—steel automatons with complex inner workings that give up brightly packaged goods to anyone with a few coins to spare. The first modern versions were used in London in the 1880s to dispense postcards and books. A few years later, they were adopted in America by the Thomas Adams Gum Company for dispensing Tutti-Frutti-flavored gum on subway platforms in New York City. The idea of an automated sales force caught on quickly, and vending machines were soon found almost everywhere. The idea perhaps reached its peak in Philadelphia with the Automat, which opened in 1902. These "waiterless" restaurants allowed patrons to buy a wide variety of foods by plunking a few coins into a box.

Today, we think of vending machines as an everyday part of our lives. Americans drop more than $30 billion a year into them, and Japan has one vending machine for every 23 of its citizens. All kinds of products—from skin care items, pajamas, and umbrellas to DVDs, iPods, ring tones, and digital cameras—can be bought without ever interacting with a salesperson.

As high-tech as all that may be, the most remarkable thing about vending machines lies not in the modern era but in the distant past. A Greek mathematician and engineer named Hero of Alexander built the very first vending machine in 215 BC! Patrons at a temple in Egypt would drop a coin into his device. Landing on one end of a lever, the heavy coin would tilt the lever upward and open a stopper that released a set quantity of holy water. When the coin slid off, the lever would return to its original position, shutting off the flow of water.

WHEN DID KITTIES GET INDOOR BATHROOM FACILITIES?

Cats have been beloved pets for thousands of years. For much of that time, though, felines were considered outdoor animals. They would often spend time in the house, but owners usually sent them packing at night. Staunch cat lovers who kept their pets indoors paid a rather smelly price, as commonly used cat box fillers such as sand, sawdust, or ashes did little to combat the notoriously rank odors that little Fluffy left behind.

In 1947, Kay Draper of Cassopolis, Michigan, found herself short of cat box filler and went to a neighbor's to see if he might have something she could use. Lucky for Kay and for cat lovers everywhere, her neighbor Ed Lowe was in the business of selling industrial absorbents, and he suggested she try some Fuller's earth—small granules of dried clay used for soaking up oil spills and such. After trying the clay, Draper raved that it was not only cleaner than other fillers she had used, but it also helped keep odors down, thanks to its tendency to chemically bind with the offending ammonia.

Smelling an opportunity, Lowe filled several paper bags with the stuff, scrawled the name "Kitty Litter" on the side, and headed to a local pet store. The owner met the idea with skepticism. Who would pay 65 cents for a bag of dirt when sand and sawdust were virtually free? Undaunted, Lowe told him to give the bags away to any customer willing to try it. Within a short time, those customers came back saying they would gladly pay for more.

Lowe spent the next few years driving around to pet stores and cat shows to promote his new product, and his diligence paid off. Today, Americans spend nearly $800 million a year on clay cat box filler—much of which goes to Lowe's company—and millions of pampered felines enjoy the luxury of indoor living.

WHO INVENTED THE JIGSAW PUZZLE?

John Spilsbury, English engraver and cartographer, that's who. In the 1760s, Mr. Spilsbury cut a wooden map of the British Empire into little pieces. Reassembling the map from the parts, he believed, would teach aristocratic schoolchildren the geographic location of imperial possessions and prepare them for eventual roles as governors and administrators. Spilsbury called his invention "Dissected Maps."

Spilsbury's "Dissected Maps" were soon popular among the wealthy classes. By the end of the 19th century, however, these "puzzles" functioned largely as an amusement. The early decades of the 20th century were the heyday of the puzzle's popularity in the United States. The first American business to produce jigsaw puzzles was Parker Brothers; the company launched its hand-cut wooden "Pastime Puzzles" in 1908. Milton Bradley followed suit with its "Premier Jig Saw Puzzles," so named because the picture, attached to a thin wooden board, was cut into curved and irregular pieces with a jigsaw. As the Great Depression came to an end in the late 1930s, inexpensive cardboard puzzles were produced at prices nearly anyone could afford.

The Big Picture

For more than a century, jigsaw puzzles have delighted people of all ages; designers are constantly at work inventing new and more difficult challenges. There are three-dimensional picture puzzles, double-sided puzzles, and puzzles with curving and irregular edges. A puzzle advertised as "the world's largest jigsaw puzzle" has 24,000 pieces. Monochromatic puzzles include "Little Red Riding Hood's Hood" (all red) and "Snow White Without the Seven Dwarfs" (all white).

WHO INVENTED TELEVISION?

Definitely Not Some Teenage Farm Boy from Idaho, Right?

Wrong. Philo T. Farnsworth, inventor of the greatest opiate the masses had ever seen, grew up on a farm in Idaho. His brilliance was obvious from an early age. In 1919, when he was only 12, he amazed his parents and older siblings by fixing a balky electrical generator on their Idaho farm. By age 14, he had built an electrical laboratory in the family attic and was setting his alarm for 4 a.m. so he could get up and read science journals for an hour before doing chores.

Farnsworth hated the unending drudgery of farmwork. He often daydreamed solutions to scientific problems while he did his chores. During the summer of 1921, he became particularly preoccupied with the possibility of transmitting moving pictures through the air.

Around the same time, big corporations like RCA were spending literally millions of research dollars trying to find a practical way to do just that. As it turned out, most of their work was focused on a theoretical dead-end. Back in 1884, German scientist Paul Nipkow had patented a device called the Nipkow disc. By rotating the disc rapidly while passing light through tiny holes, an illusion of movement could be created. In essence, the Nipkow disc was a primitive way to scan images. Farnsworth doubted that this mechanical method of scanning could ever work fast enough to send images worth watching. He was determined to find a better way.

His "Eureka!" moment came as he cultivated a field with a team of horses. Swinging the horses around to do another row, Farnsworth glanced back at the furrows behind him. Suddenly, he realized that scanning could be done electronically, line-by-line. Light could be converted into streams of electrons and then back again with such rapidity that the eye would be fooled. He immediately set about designing what would one day be called the cathode ray tube. Seven years would pass, however, before he was able to display a working model of his breakthrough.

Upon graduating from high school, Farnsworth enrolled at the University of Utah. He dropped out after only a year because he could no longer afford the tuition. Almost immediately, though, he found financial backers and moved to San Francisco to continue his research. The cathode ray tube he developed there became the basis for all television.

In 1930, a researcher from RCA named Vladimir Zworykin visited Farnsworth's California laboratory and copied his invention. When Farnsworth refused to sell his patent to RCA for $100,000, the company sued him. The legal wrangling continued for many years and, though Farnsworth eventually earned royalties from his invention, he never did get wealthy from it.

By the time Farnsworth died in 1971, there were more homes on Earth with televisions than with indoor plumbing. Ironically, the man most responsible for television appeared on the small screen only once. It was a 1957 appearance on the game show *I've Got a Secret*. Farnsworth's secret was that "I invented electric television at the age of 15." When none of the panelists guessed Farnsworth's secret, he left the studio with his winnings—$80 and a carton of Winston cigarettes.

WHERE DID EARMUFFS COME FROM?

That's right—another farm boy. Chester Greenwood was a hard-working kid from Farmington, Maine, who endured a typical hardscrabble childhood in rural New England. Disciplined and diligent, he dropped out of school to help his large family by working on the farm and trekking eight or more miles to deliver eggs and fudge to his neighbors. This was one of the few occasions when he had the opportunity to indulge in the fun that led to his fortune.

A Cool Idea

In the winter of 1873, the 15-year-old headed to a nearby pond to try out a new pair of ice skates. Before he reached his destination, he had to turn back because the bitter cold was hurting his ears. Determined to go skating, Greenwood took a piece of baling wire he found around the farm and formed a loop at each end. He brought the wire and some beaver fur to his grandmother and asked her to sew the material onto the loops. Then he slipped the device over his head.

Getting Warmer

Young Chester never had to worry about cold ears—or making his first million—again. His "Greenwood Champion Ear Protector" eventually became the familiar winter item we call earmuffs—but only after a few more years of tinkering. Unsatisfied with the loose fit of the original design, Greenwood improved his invention by using a wide steel band instead of wire. This allowed him to add hinges where the band connected to the muff, so the fabric could fit snugly against the ears and the device could be folded when not in use.

Chester earned a patent for the revised design in 1877 at the age of 18 and then opened a factory near his hometown. His business became a central part of Farmington's economy, and it remains the largest producer of earmuffs in the world.

WHO INVENTED THE SWISS ARMY KNIFE?

A Swiss farm boy, you say? Not quite. The distinctive multitool pocketknife was the brainchild of Swiss cutlery manufacturer Karl Elsener. A true patriot, Elsener bristled at the fact that Swiss soldiers got their standard-issue knives from a German manufacturer, and he set out to win the contract from his government. In the 1890s, he designed a unique spring mechanism for pocketknives that allowed the handle to hold several blades.

That was clever enough in and of itself, but Elsener's true moment of genius came when he decided that rather than adding extra blades, he would include several basic tools in his knife—a can opener, a hole punch, and a screwdriver. According to some sources, it was the screwdriver that won over the Swiss military brass; the nation's infantry had just begun using a new type of rifle, and soldiers needed screwdrivers to perform basic maintenance on the weapon.

Elsener dubbed his creation the "Soldier's Knife" and followed it up with a lightweight version with a few more tools called the "Officer's and Sports Knife." Before long, handymen around the world were carrying them in their pockets, but it wasn't until World War II—when American GIs dubbed it the Swiss Army Knife—that the tool got the name we use today.

Elsener's company, Victorinox, is still in business, producing thousands of knives a day in some 300 configurations. Almost any tool you can imagine can be found on one model or another: corkscrew, wire strippers, toothpick, fish scaler, ruler, nail file, saw, chisel, magnifying glass, flashlight—even a ballpoint pen or a tracheotomy knife!

HOW WAS THE PRINTING PRESS INVENTED?

Sure, Johannes Gutenberg's development of the printing press in 15th-century Germany led to mass-market publishing. But innovations in printing technology were around long before Gutenberg revolutionized the industry. Although printing is usually associated with reading materials, the original impetus behind printing technology was the need to create identical copies of the same thing. Printing actually began with coining, when centralized states branded their coins with uniform numbers and symbols.

In those days, written manuscripts were copied the old-fashioned way, letter by letter, by hand. Only the upper echelons of society were literate, books were costly, and the laborious and artistic method of copying matched the rarity of books.

The first major innovation in printing came with the Chinese invention of block printing by the eighth century AD. Block printing involved carving letters or images into a surface, inking that surface, and pressing it on to paper, parchment, or cloth. The method was used for a variety of purposes, from decorating clothes to copying religious scrolls. The blocks were usually made of wood, which posed a problem as the wood eventually decayed or cracked. Oftentimes entire pages of a manuscript, complete with illustrations, were carved into a single block that could be used again and again.

The Chinese also invented movable type, which would prove to be the prerequisite to efficient printing presses. Movable type is faster than block printing because individual characters, usually letters or punctuation, are created by being cast into molds. Once this grab bag of individual characters is made, they can then be reused and rearranged in infinite combinations by changing the typeset. Movable type characters are also more uniform than the carved letters of block printing. Pi-Sheng invented this method in 1045 using clay molds. The method spread to Korea and Japan, and metal movable type was created in Korea by 1230.

Supply and Demand

The Chinese didn't use movable type extensively because their language consists of thousands of characters, and movable type makes printing efficient only in a language with fewer letters, like the English alphabet's 26. Meanwhile, Europeans used the imported concept of block printing to make popular objects like playing cards or illustrated children's books. During the Middle Ages, serious secular scholarship had all but disappeared in Europe, and the reproduction of new and classical texts was mostly confined to the Asian and Arab worlds.

The catalyst for change was the growth of literacy. As it spread among the middle classes, lay people, especially in Germany, showed an interest in reading religious texts for themselves. Thus, German entrepreneur Johannes Gutenberg, the son of a coin minter, began to experiment with metal movable type pieces. It's believed Gutenberg was unfamiliar with the previously invented Chinese method, but at any rate, several other Europeans were experimenting with similar methods at the same time as Gutenberg.

By the 1440s, Gutenberg had set up a printing shop in Mainz, Germany, and in 1450, he set out to produce a Bible. Gutenberg perfected several printing methods, such as right justification, and preferred alloys in the production of metal types. By 1455, Gutenberg's press had produced 200 copies of his Bible—quite the feat at the time, considering one Bible could take years to copy by hand. These Bibles were sold for less than hand-copied ones yet were still expensive enough for profit margins equivalent to modern-day millions.

Printing presses were soon popping up all across Europe. By 1499, an estimated 15 million books had been produced by at least 1,000 printing presses, mostly in Germany and then throughout Italy. For the first time ever, ideas were not only dreamed up and written down—they were efficiently reproduced and spread over long distances. The proliferation of these first German printing presses is commonly credited with the end of the Middle Ages and the dawn of the Renaissance.

HOW DID WE GET THE MODERN DRUM SET?

Sure, individual drums of all kinds have been around for thousands of years, but how did all those cool pieces assemble themselves into the noisemaking monster ensemble that can now be heard in concert halls and suburban basements across the world?

It started with vaudeville, some time around the end of the 19th century. Live bands were an essential part of American theater productions, and they were soon to become important in silent movie theaters as well. A band might employ three drummers: one to play snare drum, one to play bass drum, and one to play cymbals. But there was often very little stage space to set up equipment, so drummers invented ways of closely stacking drums. They also began learning how to play more than one instrument at the same time.

In 1909, vaudeville drummer William Ludwig designed a spring-loaded bass drum foot pedal that could handle the fast tempos he needed to play. This allowed quick foot control and freed his hands to play other drums. His invention caught on with other drummers. Early drum sets featured Ludwig's bass drum and foot pedal, a snare drum mounted on a stand, and other percussion instruments like cymbals, cowbells, whistles, chimes, and wood blocks fixed on a tray above the bass drum. Musicians soon began attaching special mounting arms to their bass drums to hold additional drums. After a while, cymbals got their own stands.

In the early days of the drum set, drummers sometimes used a simple pair of foot cymbals to help them keep time. This device evolved into the first "low boy"—a spring-operated mechanism that opened and closed the cymbals and stood about a foot high. By the late 1920s, this design had been improved upon, and an early version of the hi-hat was being used. The hi-hat allowed drummers to keep time on a cymbal with either their hands or their feet. The final piece of the modern drum set had arrived.

WHO INVENTED THE POTATO CHIP?

If you can't eat just one potato chip, blame it on the well-named chef George Crum. He reportedly created the all-American salty snack in 1853 at Moon's Lake House near Saratoga Springs, New York. Exasperated with a customer who continuously sent his fried potatoes back, complaining that they were soggy and not crunchy enough, Crum sliced the potatoes as thin as possible, fried them in hot grease, then doused them liberally with salt. The customer loved them and "Saratoga Chips" quickly became a popular item at the lodge and throughout New England.

Eventually, the chips were mass-produced for individual home consumption, but since they were stored in barrels or tins, they quickly went stale. Then, in the 1920s, Laura Scudder invented the airtight bag by ironing together two pieces of waxed paper, thus keeping the chips fresh longer. Today, chips are packaged in plastic or foil bags or cardboard containers and come in a variety of flavors, including sour cream and onion, barbecue, and salt and vinegar.

Salty Addendum

And while we're on the subject of sodium-laden delights, we can thank a frustrated teacher with leftover bread dough for the invention of the soft pretzel. In AD 610, while baking bread, an Italian monk decided to create a treat to motivate his distracted catechism students. He rolled out ropes of dough, twisted them around to resemble hands crossed on the chest in prayer, and baked them.

The monk christened his snacks *pretiola*, Latin for "little reward." Parents who tasted their children's classroom treats referred to them as brachiola, or "little arms." When pretiola arrived in Germany, they were called bretzels.

HAVE CANADIANS EVER INVENTED ANYTHING USEFUL?

Hold on a minute—there's no reason to hate on the Great White North. Even Canadians themselves might be surprised by how many inventions they've racked up. It's a lot more than Alexander Graham Bell's telephone.

Automatic postal sorter (Dr. Maurice Levy, 1956):
Revolutionizing mail delivery, his first model processed 30,000 letters an hour with an average of three errors. By 1957, a model was processing approximately 200,000 letters per hour.

Basketball (James Naismith, 1891): What most don't know is that the Ontarian invented the game to keep kids out of trouble. Teaching at a Massachusetts YMCA school, the Canadian pedagogue believed that a noncontact indoor sport would do wonders for kids' behavior.

Electric car heater (Thomas Ahearn, 1890): This one makes a lot of sense, considering the tender mercies of Canadian winters. It was one of this Ottawan's many patents relating to electric heat, including a hot water heater and an iron.

Electric lightbulb (Henry Woodward and Mathew Evans, 1874): These Canadians paved the way for Thomas Edison's later improvements to the lightbulb. Their early models were glass cylinders with carbon rods positioned between electrodes. The cylinders were filled with nitrogen. When they failed to sell the lightbulbs commercially, they sold their patent to Edison.

Flight suit (Dr. Wilbur Franks, 1941): This anti-gravity suit enabled combat pilots to withstand G-force pressure and extreme acceleration.

Hydrofoil boat (Alexander Graham Bell/Casey Baldwin, 1908): Fact: water's drag slows down boats. In the early days of aviation, Bell and Baldwin wondered: what if you could mount a wing under a boat? The wing lifted the hull out of the water, improving both the speed and the ride.

Insulin process (Sir Frederick Banting, et. al., 1922):
His team pioneered the understanding of insulin's central role in diabetes, then learned to produce it from the pancreas of a cow. Through injections, diabetics could now regulate their conditions. Banting's group deserves special credit for placing the invention into the public domain rather than making a lot of money with it.

Java (James Gosling, 1994): This Alberta native created the Java programming language. Most people think of Java as it relates to the Internet, but it's also found in devices as diverse as the Mars Rover, toasters, cars, and industrial-inventory tagging, to name a few.

Paint roller (Norman Breakey, 1940): Breakey was a victim of the legal system. He invented this useful painting method but didn't have the capital to defend his patent from those eager to make money from his idea. This may explain why he also invented a beer keg tap.

Plastic garbage bag (Henry Wasylyk, 1950): Family lore has it that Wasylyk invented it out of revenge, to compete with a company that had offered Prairie farmers (including Wasylyk) ruinously low prices for their wheat during the Depression. In any case, Union Carbide bought Wasylyk's idea, profitably.

Rotary snowplow (Dr. J. W. Elliott, 1869): Consider the difficulties to be surmounted while building a railroad across a country with snowy winters. How many people had to shovel off several thousand miles of track several months per year? Dr. Elliott, a dentist by trade, devised a fan to enable the locomotive to plow the snow itself.

Snowblower (Arthur Sicard, 1925): As a Quebecois farm boy, Sicard knew that keeping cows fed in a snowy environment was a challenge to other farmers. He also knew that snowstorm-blocked roads caused a lot of dairy spoilage. After studying how grain threshers worked in the late nineteenth century, he began developing prototypes that would move snow instead. After 25 winters of experimentation, he unveiled the first "snowblowing" device in 1925. It was essentially a truck with a fanlike snowblower in front. The walk-behind snowblower didn't come along until the 1950s, by which time Sicard's machines were working busily on the streets and roads of Canada.

Wonderbra (Louise Poirier, 1964):
Poirier developed it while working for Canadelle, a company well known to Canadian women for more than half a century of firm support. The Wonderbra name dates back to the 1930s, but Poirier pushed the bustline maximizer version to market in 1964.

1. Thomas Edison invented one of the following. Which was it?
a. Photographic film
b. Automatic paper towel dispenser
c. Electrographic vote recorder
d. Internal combustion engine

2. Who invented the fountain pen?
a. Immanuel Kant
b. Eli Whitney
c. Petrache Poenaru
d. Thomas Edison

3. What did Alfred Nobel invent?
a. Dynamite
b. The washing machine
c. Bubble gum
d. The machine gun

4. Along with stoves, lightning rods, and other useful devices, Ben Franklin invented this.
a. Bifocals
b. Waterproof shoes
c. Ping pong
d. All of the above

5. Who invented the computer mouse?
a. Alan Turing
b. Freeman Dyson
c. Bill Gates
d. Douglas Engelbart

6. This famous product was repurposed from a wallpaper-cleaning compound concocted by Noah McVicker.
a. Play-Doh
b. Superglue
c. Mustard gas
d. Bondo

7. 11-year-old Frank Epperson accidentally invented this sweet treat.
a. Ice cream
b. Jawbreaker
c. Popsicle
d. Cotton candy

8. While experimenting with the gas tetrafluoroethylene, Roy Plunkett accidentally invented this.
a. Plastic
b. Teflon
c. Stainless steel
d. Graphene

9. Buckminster Fuller popularized the geodesic dome, but which engineer designed one first?
a. Gustave Eiffel
b. Walther Bauersfeld
c. Henry Ford
d. Wernher von Braun

10. Nikola Tesla invented:
a. The Tesla Roadster
b. A cold fusion battery
c. A remote-controlled model boat
d. The light bulb

1.
c. Electrographic vote recorder

2.
c. Petrache Poenaru

3.
a. Dynamite

4.
a. Bifocals

5.
d. Douglas Engelbart

6.
a. Play-Doh

7.
c. Popsicle

8.
b. Teflon

9.
b. Walther Bauersfeld

10.
c. A remote-controlled model boat

HOW TO DO
ALARMING THINGS

It's nice to have an edgy skill that no one else has, isn't it? Something that sets you apart—a bit of morally ambivalent proficiency that says to others, "I spent serious time learning how to do this—what else might lurk in my wheelhouse?"

How many of your friends can shrink a head? Hypnotize a chicken? Probably none. But you on the other hand will soon have the wherewithal to escape quicksand and fit ships into bottles. And if you ever need to marry a significant other while one of you is incarcerated, you'll be prepared for that too.

CAN YOU REALLY BREAK A CONCRETE BLOCK WITH YOUR HAND?

A Classic of Martial Arts Showmanship—How the Heck Is It Possible?

In a face-off between hand and block, the hand has a surprising advantage: bone is significantly stronger than concrete. In fact, bone can withstand about 40 times more stress than concrete before reaching its breaking point. What's more, the surrounding muscles and ligaments in your hands are good stress absorbers, making the hand and arm one tough weapon. So if you position your hand correctly, you're not going to break it by hitting concrete.

The trick to smashing a block is thrusting this sturdy mass into the concrete with enough force to bend the block beyond its breaking point. The force of any impact is determined by the momentum of the two objects in the collision. Momentum is a multiple of the mass and velocity of an object.

Velocity Is the Key

When striking an object, the speed of your blow is critical. You also have to hit the block with a relatively small area of your hand, so that the force of the impact is focused in one spot on the block—this concentrates the stress on the concrete. As in golf, the only way for a martial arts student to hit accurately with greater speed is practice, practice, practice. But there is a basic mental trick involved: you have to overcome your natural instinct to slow your strike as your hand approaches the block.

Martial arts masters concentrate on an impact spot beyond the block, so that the hand is still at maximum speed when it makes contact with the concrete.

Body Mass Counts Too

You also need to put as much body mass as you can into the strike; this can be achieved by twisting your body and lowering your torso as you make contact. A black belt in karate can throw a chop at about 46 feet per second, which results in a force of about 2,800 newtons. (A newton is the unit of force needed to accelerate a mass.) That's more than enough chopping power to break the standard one-and-a-half-inch concrete slabs that are commonly used in demonstrations and typically can withstand only 1,900 newtons.

Nonetheless, while hands are dandy in a block-breaking exhibition, you'll find that for sidewalk demolition and other large projects, jackhammers are really the way to go.

HOW DO I MARRY A PRISON INMATE?

A great question, and if it's on your need-to-know checklist, it's probably in between How to Live with Recidivism and How to Find and Replace Serial Numbers. All rules and regulations will vary from prison to prison and state to state. However, generally speaking, there are a few provisos that should be followed—and maybe a little and soul searching too. After all, the divorce rate for a spouse incarcerated for more than a year is 85 percent.

Request a Marriage Packet: The betrothed inmate needs specific marriage request forms. In order to jailhouse rock accordingly, both parties will have to fill out the forms completely and have the appropriate amount of money available through a money order.

Have All Required Documentation: Proper identification, proof of age and citizenship, and all the necessary forms from the prison need to be polished and completed.

Find and Keep the Correct Prison Contact: Mainly done through the prison's family visitation coordinator, each couple should remain well connected to the person who will make sure all t's have been crossed and i's have been dotted.

Make Arrangements with Officiant: Most prisons will have a list of approved pastors, as well as their own provided chaplain, who can offer succinct advice. (This ain't his/her first rodeo.)

Witness Needed: Like all marriages, someone is required to be present to provide proof that this match is, in fact, legally binding.

Other Costs and Fees: And like all the best things in life, love—legally speaking, of course—isn't free. Couples considering inmate matrimony will also need to make sure they have all their mandatory state debts paid in full. Well, minus the time served.

HOW DO I ESCAPE QUICKSAND?

This is a crucial skill for those times when you need to take a shortcut through the jungle to avoid drug lords, fanatical revolutionaries, or Canadian tourists. If you happen to get trapped in one of nature's suction pits, hang loose. Crack some jokes ("We seem to have gotten bogged down, Miss Toffington"). And don't start thrashing around in a panic.

Let's say you're running through the woods and you trip and fall. As you attempt to right yourself, you realize that the earth below you isn't really earth at all, and you find it impossible to find purchase. You are wet and covered in a granular grime, but it's not a body of water or sand pit that you've fallen into. This substance seems more like a combination of the two. In fact, it is—you have fallen into a quicksand pit. What you do from this point forth will determine whether this will be a momentary inconvenience or just a slightly longer inconvenience.

A Quicksand Primer

Quicksand is a sand, silt, or clay pit that has become hydrated, which reduces its viscosity. Therefore, when a person is "sucked" down, they are simply sinking as they would in any body of water.

So why does quicksand make people so nervous? It's probably due to the fact that it can present resistance to the person who steps in it. This is particularly true of someone who is wearing heavy boots, laden with a backpack, or can hear the shouts of gun-touting maniacs in the distance.

It's All in the Legs

In the human thirst for drama and/or comedy, quicksand has a reputation as a substance to be reckoned with. Television sitcoms like *Gilligan's Island* and films like *The Princess Bride* portrayed quicksand as a dangerous and potentially deadly obstacle. But the facts show something far different. Because quicksand is denser than water, it allows for easy floating. If you stumble into a pit, you will sink only up to your chest or shoulders. If you want to escape, all you need to do is move your legs slowly. This action will create a space through which water will flow, thereby loosening the sand's grip. You should then be able to float on your back until the heat-maddened guerillas arrive.

HOW DO I HYPNOTIZE A CHICKEN?

Gently hold the chicken on its side on a flat surface, lightly securing its head. Move either your index finger or a small stick back and forth in front of the bird, about four or five inches from its beak. Keep the motion parallel to its head. Soon, the bird will fall into a "trance," which is easily lifted when you release the chicken.

HOW DO I SHRINK A HEAD?

Those Wacky Jivaro

Well into the 20th century, the Amazonian Jivaro tribe made a point of returning from battle toting the shrunken heads of its enemies. Talk about unique souvenirs.

These heads, or *tsantsa*, were a central element of the Jivaro practice of blood revenge. If someone from a neighboring tribe—or even a different group within the Jivaro tribe— wronged your family, it was essential that you exact revenge on his kin. The result was a cycle of murder, head collection, and hurt feelings.

Not only was tsantsa the best revenge, but it was also the best way to prevent supernatural harassment from your victim. The Jivaro believed that shrinking the victim's head captured his soul, keeping him from moving on to the afterlife, where he could torment you and your dead ancestors.

The Process

The Jivaro decapitated the offending party—or one of his relatives—and looped a band through the head's mouth and neck hole, making a sort of handle. Then they high-tailed it to a secluded camp by a river, where they sliced open the back of the head, carefully peeled away the skin, and tossed the skull into the river as an offering to a spirit they believed lived in the anaconda snake.

Next, they sewed the eyes shut, fastened the mouth closed with wooden skewers, and placed the head in boiling water for up to two hours. The boiling process shrank the head to about a third of its normal size. After boiling, the Jivaro began the trip back home, continuing to work on the tsantsa along the way.

They turned the skin inside out and scraped away any remaining flesh before turning it right-side out and sewing up the back of the head. The Jivaron then put scorching rocks inside the head and filled and refilled it with hot sand, drying the skin and shrinking it further. Next, they removed the skewers from the lips and tied them shut with long lengths of string.

The head then was hung over a fire for hardening and blackening and was covered in charcoal to seal in the spirit of the dead individual. Finally, the Jivaro cut a hole in the top of the head and inserted a stick with a loop of sturdy string tied to it. And there it was: a perfect shrunken head to wear around the neck.

From Trophies to Toys

Back home, the tsantsa were the centerpieces of several feasts. The shrinking process and the feasts were essential requirements for exacting revenge. After that purpose was served, however, the heads no longer were important and often ended up as toys for kids.

The tribe even set up a profitable side business, trading the heads to foreigners for guns and other goods, but the Peruvian and Ecuadorian governments cracked down on the practice in the 1930s and 1940s. Party poopers.

HOW DO I TRAIN MY SIGNIFICANT OTHER?

Behavioral Basics

It's a fact: the science of psychology is the basis of most animal training. It's no secret that humans are animals, and, sure enough, the same kinds of techniques that work on pets can be used on people.

Behavioral psychology is the study of observable actions and responses. Most theories assume animals are born as "blank slates"; they are later shaped by their interactions with the environment. In its most basic form, this means we tend to repeat actions with positive consequences and avoid actions with negative consequences.

Seems simple enough, right? This sort of thinking is nothing new: for years, spouses have taken this approach to change their loved ones' behavior. Sandra Dee takes this approach with her husband, played by Bobby Darin, in the 1963 movie *If a Man Answers*. In it, her mother hands her a dog training manual and advises that what will work for the pooch will work for the hubby. Now, let's break down the core principles and see how they can work for you.

Understanding Reinforcement

The foundation of most animal training starts with the idea of reinforcement—something that increases a desired behavior. It could be positive: the addition of something to the environment, such as food or a belly rub. It could also be negative: the removal of something desirable from the environment, or a loud noise or disapproving look. Either can work, as long as the animal learns to associate the reinforcement with the behavior you're trying to teach. Now, let's put it into action.

Learning a Behavior: The Lazy Dog

In our first example, let's say we have a dog that won't go into its doghouse. Our initial thought might be to put a treat in the doghouse doorway to coax it inside. This, however, isn't likely to work; the dog will just grab the treat and dart away. Why? Because it's bribery, not reinforcement. Remember, reinforcement has to be linked with a specific behavior.

The trainer's answer is to ignore the dog while it's avoiding the house, and then reinforce it with the treat when it finally ventures inside on its own. The pup now knows a treat appeared because of what it did, and the behavior has been learned.

Learning a Behavior: The Lazy Boyfriend

Put this into a relationship setting: let's say you want your boyfriend to dress up more often. Nagging him about it isn't likely to work in the long-term. The trick, then, is to avoid complimenting him or giving him extra attention on the nights he dresses like a slob. Then, on a night when he dresses nicely, you lay on the praise. Tell him with enthusiasm how great he looks, and—if you want to really reinforce it—give him some kind of special reward as soon as you get home. We'll leave it up to you to decide what the reward should be.

Maintaining a Behavior: The Dancing Dolphin

All right, the behavior's been learned—now it's time to maintain it. You may think the best thing would be to present a reward every time you see the behavior, but animal trainers have learned otherwise. They've found the more effective technique is what's called a variable schedule of reinforcement.

Think about it: a dolphin trainer won't usually give the animal a treat after every trick. Instead, the trainer will randomly reinforce the good behavior, giving the dolphin a treat on, say, the first, third, and sixth trick. That way the dolphin is more likely to keep working hard for the reward, since it can't anticipate when it'll come, as opposed to thinking it can get lazy and do the absolute minimum to get the treat that comes every time.

Maintaining a Behavior: The Dancing Husband

It's no surprise that many men don't favor the dance floor. But once you've helped your husband learn the behavior (using the technique you learned above), you can keep him boogying by using the same kind of variable reinforcement used with the dolphin. In a similar scenario, after the second night of dancing, go easy on the compliments and rewards. Like the dolphin trainer, if you lay it on thick every time, your hubby is going to realize he doesn't have to work hard to get his reinforcement. But if on, say, the third, fifth, and eighth nights, you deliver the full reward again, you'll enjoy continued success.

Stopping a Behavior: The Barking Dog

A barking dog is extremely annoying. But by using negative reinforcement, a trainer can teach it to keep quiet. Animals don't like having bright lights shone in their faces, so a trainer might use that tactic as the unwanted addition to the environment.

Every time the dog barks, he or she shines a bright light at it. As soon as the barking stops, the light goes off. Give it enough time, and the dog will learn what's happening and modify its behavior accordingly.

Stopping a Behavior: The Barking Boyfriend

Tired of dealing with your mate's horrible mood when he comes home from work every night? Try the same concept, but with more subtle tactics. When he starts getting cross with you, leave the room or stop responding to his mood. When he takes on a more pleasant tone, return to normal. He'll subconsciously make the connection.

That's just the start of how you can put animal training techniques to use in your personal life. Take the time to understand motivation and you can, within reason, have a lot more pull over people than you realize. Remember, it's all about reinforcement, no matter how small the gesture.

WHAT'S THE CORRECT WAY TO MAKE A MARTINI?

Hint: James Bond Was Wrong

Ah, the martini, that quintessential American symbol of class, elegance, and alcoholism. Journalist H. L. Mencken called it "the only American invention as perfect as a sonnet." Historian Bernard DeVoto opined that the martini is "the supreme American gift to world culture"—a sad testament to America's cultural legacy, if true (taking nothing away from the martini, of course). Winston Churchill and Franklin Roosevelt were known for sipping martinis as they went about defeating the Nazis and salvaging our civilization. But perhaps nobody did as much for the martini as fictional agent James Bond, who made the drink synonymous with debonair elegance. And we all know the recipe that Mr. Bond demanded from his bartenders: vodka, straight up, very cold, and—always, always—shaken, not stirred.

As it turns out, 007 might know a great deal about wearing tuxedos, using ingenious gadgets, and getting female foreign agents to bend to his will, but when it comes to the martini, he's a bit of a rube. According to tradition, a martini is made with gin and is always stirred.

Why Stirring Is the Way to Go

There are good reasons why a martini should only be stirred. Most mixologists agree that shaking should be reserved for cloudy drinks—cocktails made with fruit juice, dairy products, or eggs—and that clear drinks should usually be stirred. The ingredients in a cloudy drink require more thorough mixing; vigorous shaking does a better job of blending them than stirring. Meanwhile, clarity is an important part of a clear drink's presentation; shaking it causes air bubbles to form, which makes it less appealing to the eye.

But it's more than a matter of presentation. When a bartender mixes a drink, he's not just blending the ingredients—he's also chilling them with chunks of ice, which are typically strained out when the cocktail is poured. As the ice cools the drink during the mixing process, it begins to melt; this adds a small amount of water to the recipe.

This "watering down" is desirable as long as it's strictly controlled, because it helps to temper the bite of the liquor. Shaking a drink rather than stirring it results in a colder, more watery finished product. These qualities can sometimes enhance a cocktail, but in a drink like a martini—which is simply a precisely measured blend of gin and vermouth—a little extra water can be ruinous. It's obvious, based on this, that martinis need to be stirred.

HOW DO YOU BECOME A SAINT?

Everyone who has worked in an office environment has encountered that guy who thinks he should be a saint. You know, the only person who ever fills the copy machine with paper? The benevolent soul—the only one, to hear him tell it— who respects his coworkers enough to clean up after himself in the break room? Yeah, that guy. He should be a saint, right?

With apologies to Bob from Human Resources, becoming a saint is quite a bit more complicated than being punctual for staff meetings. Though most religions throughout history have honored particularly holy members in different ways, most people think of sainthood—at least in Western culture—in terms of Roman Catholicism. In the Catholic Church, the process of becoming a saint is known as canonization.

Though sainthood is the ultimate honor in the Catholic Church, good Christians destined to become saints won't know it during their lifetime—canonization starts after the candidate has died. In fact, there usually is a five-year waiting period after death before the Catholic Church will consider a candidate for sainthood. Once the waiting period is finished, local church officials will study the life and writings of the proposed saint to make sure that he or she lived a truly Christian life. If the person passes muster, the pope labels him or her "venerable."

The next step in canonization involves attributing a miracle— like spontaneous healings at the candidate's grave or appearances of holy images—to the now-venerable candidate. (Sorry, Bob, filing your TPS report by deadline doesn't count.) Once the church determines that the miracle in question can be attributed to the candidate, that person is "beatified."

However, beatification still isn't enough to become a saint. Because anyone can get lucky and cure a paraplegic once— look, even a blind squirrel can stumble upon one nut—the church requires a second miracle to ensure that the first wasn't a fluke. Only after this second miracle is confirmed is the candidate officially made a saint.

There is a quicker way to sainthood—martyrdom. So if Bob from HR really wants to become a saint, there are probably plenty of volunteers who would help him along that path.

HOW DO YOU MAKE A CITIZEN'S ARREST?

Nearly every state allows an ordinary person to make a citizen's arrest, but this doesn't mean that you should convert your garage into a jail and start rounding up suspected criminals. Perp-busting is best left to professionals.

The concept of a citizen's arrest dates to medieval England, where it was standard practice for ordinary people to help maintain order by apprehending and detaining anyone who was observed committing a crime. This remained part of English common law, and over the years, the concept spread to other countries. Standards of exactly what citizens could and couldn't do to detain suspected criminals were modified over the years, as well.

Today, laws governing citizen's arrests vary from country to country; in the United States, they vary from state to state. The intent is to give law-abiding citizens the power to stop someone from inflicting harm when there's no time to wait for authorities. It's considered a last resort and is only meant for dire emergencies.

Every state except North Carolina explicitly grants citizens (and, generally, other residents) the power to arrest someone who is seen committing a felony. Some states extend this to allow a citizen's arrest when the citizen has probable cause to believe that someone has committed a felony.

"Arrest" in this context means stopping and detaining the suspect until law enforcement arrives. Kentucky law kicks it up a notch—it grants citizens the right to use deadly force to stop a fleeing suspected felon.

The general guidelines for a citizen's arrest in the United States break down like this: in most cases, you can arrest someone during or immediately following the commission of a criminal act. First, you tell the suspect to stop what he or she is doing, and then you announce that you're making a citizen's arrest. As long as the suspect stays put, you don't have the right to physically restrain him or her.

Don't notify the suspect of his or her constitutional rights; this would be considered impersonating an officer. Typically, you don't have the right to search or interrogate a suspect, either. If the suspect resists, you have the right to use enough force to detain him or her until law enforcement arrives. It's illegal to use excessive force or to imprison someone extendedly if either is due to your failure to notify law enforcement immediately.

Even if you follow the law to the letter, making a citizen's arrest is risky business because, among other reasons, the law doesn't grant you the same legal protection it gives a police officer. In most cases, the suspect could sue you personally for false arrest or false imprisonment, especially if he or she ends up being acquitted of the charges. In other words, if you see a fishy-looking character running down the street, think twice before you spring into action and yell, "Stop!"

HOW DO YOU PUT A SHIP IN A BOTTLE?

Ask Very Nicely and Tell It to Suck in Its Gut, of Course

Actually, for reasons we believe have to do with a lack television, video games, and frisbees, people have been putting stuff in empty bottles for centuries.

Before ships caught on, "patience bottles" were filled with scenes of religious imagery (Jesus on the cross, for example), and the aptly named "mining bottles" had multilevel scenes of ore mining (oh, the excitement of those days). The earliest mining bottle, which probably dates to 1719, was created by Matthias Buchinger, a well-known "entertainer" of the time who had no arms or legs. Mining bottles originated in what is now Hungary.

People started shoving ships into bottles in the mid- to late eighteenth century. Most people did not write the dates on their creations, and since many pieces were made with old bottles that had been sitting around, the date on the actual bottle doesn't necessarily correlate with when the ship was put in it. The earliest known ship in a bottle that someone bothered to date (on the sails) was constructed in 1784.

Bottling ships really caught on in the 1830s, when clear glass became more common. It is still a popular hobby these days, with clubs and associations around the world devoted to the skill.

But how do you get that boat into the bottle? Cut the bottle in half, put the ship in, and then seal it back up using glue and trained ants? It's actually pretty simple (not easy, but simple). You need some skill—and a lot of patience. The hull (or bottom of the boat) is narrow enough to fit through the neck of the bottle. The masts are hinged so that they can be pushed flat against the hull. While the ship is outside the bottle, the sails are attached and a string is tied to the mast.

The masts and sails are bent so that they are flat, and then the whole thing is pushed through the bottleneck. Glue or putty on the bottom of the bottle keeps the ship anchored. Once the ship is in, a long tool, shaped like a rod or skewer, is used to position it. Finally, the string that is attached to the masts is pulled to bring up the sails and complete the illusion.

There are some types of boats—motorboats, for example—that are too wide to get into the bottle in one piece. These are assembled inside the bottle using rods, which takes a lot of patience and a steady hand.

Getting a ship out of a bottle? Easy—navigate it toward an iceberg or a jagged rock.

1. In order to run for president, you must:
a. Belong to a political party
b. Be at least 35 years old
c. Prove you were born in the United States
d. Be able to recite the Constitution

2. On average, how long can you survive without water?
a. About a month
b. About three weeks
c. About two weeks
d. About three days

3. Gunpowder is made with charcoal, sulfur, and this.
a. Salt
b. Chlorine
c. Potassium citrate
d. Potassium nitrate

4. How long do you age the classic Chinese thousand-year egg?
a. One thousand years
b. One hundred years
c. A couple of months
d. A couple of days

5. To make dynamite, you need to include this.
a. Nitroglycerin
b. Aluminum
c. Uranium
d. Plutonium

6. Which food will last the longest?
a. Spelt
b. Quinoa
c. Cornmeal
d. Olive oil

7. On average, how long can you survive without air?
a. About a month
b. About three days
c. About three hours
d. About three minutes

8. Who holds the record for the highest parachute jump (135,890 feet)?
a. Joseph William Kittinger II
b. Alan Eustace
c. Felix Baumgartner
d. Yevgeni Andreyev

9. Which ingredient is essential for making beer?
a. Rice
b. Fruit juice
c. Yeast
d. Grass

10. To become a secret service agent, you must:
a. Be able to see in the dark
b. Possess a bachelor's degree
c. Know the position of the stars during the day
d. Be born in the United States

1.
b. Be at least 35 years old

2.
d. About three days

3.
d. Potassium nitrate

4.
c. A couple of months

5.
a. Nitroglycerin

6.
a. Spelt

7.
d. About three minutes

8.
b. Alan Eustace

9.
c. Yeast

10.
b. Possess a bachelor's degree

PESSIMISM

LIFE IS UNFAIR . . . HORRIBLY UNFAIR

Cheer up, Eeyore, and enjoy a chapter custom-made for pessimists like you. You, with your morbid fascination with the endless failures of Wile E. Coyote, poisoned Halloween candy, plagues, and killer asteroids, will find much conversational fodder herein. Disease, prison, injustice, doom and ruination—it can all be found here. And since you're always bringing up Murphy the minute something goes wrong, we thought it would be nice to conclude with a little background on who he was and how he came to be associated with that law.

DO COFFINS COME WITH LIFETIME GUARANTEES?

How long does a coffin last? Some, like the sarcophagi of the ancient Egyptians, can hold up for centuries. Others, like the Ecopod, a coffin made of recycled newspapers by a British company of the same name, are intended to biodegrade within a few years.

Has any coffin maker offered a lifetime guarantee? Tough question—the best we could find are rumors. People in Indiana have claimed that the state's Batesville Casket Company used to sell caskets with lifetime guarantees, but the company wouldn't confirm this assertion.

Like many casket manufacturers, the Batesville company produces waterproof caskets that are guaranteed not to leak for between twenty and seventy-five years, depending on the price of the casket. Perhaps at one time an overeager funeral director assured grieving families that the deluxe seventy-five-year, leak-proof model would keep their dearly departed safe for at least a lifetime, "guaranteed."

When arranging a funeral, it helps to remember that only the coffin can be guaranteed to last, not the body inside. In fact, the more airtight the coffin, the more rapidly a corpse will disintegrate due to the activity of anaerobic microbes. These bacteria, which thrive in the absence of oxygen, can literally liquefy a dead body. With a little fresh air, a body will decay more slowly. But fast or slow, nature decrees that all bodies inevitably decay, no matter how fancy the coffin.

WHY DO MOSQUITOES BITE SOME PEOPLE MORE THAN OTHERS?

Are Some Folks Just More Delicious?

One theory suggests that mosquitoes are picky eaters that choose potential victims based on blood type. Eighty-five percent of humans secrete a chemical marker through their pores that indicates their blood type. In some cases, the marker hits the mosquito the same way the smell of fresh-baked bread hits human nostrils. Microscopic drops of saliva form around the insect's proboscis, the little devil hits the smorgasbord, and it digs in as soon as it feels safe.

A study conducted in 2004 showed that mosquitoes land on individuals with Type O blood more often than they feast on those with any other blood type. Conversely, Type A appears to be the least popular flavor for mosquitoes. The fortunate 15 percent of humanity whose pores do not secrete a blood-type marker suffer the fewest bites; like a roadside diner with a burned-out neon sign, they attract hardly any customers at all.

In 2006, scientists performed a test using a Y-shaped tube. Two individuals stuck a hand in the tube, and mosquitoes that were released into the tube could choose which hand to bite. Scientists collected perspiration from the person who attracted the fewest mosquitoes to study its chemical makeup. Researchers also believe that some people may emit a masking odor that actually repels mosquitoes. By studying the chemicals these lucky people excrete, scientists hope to create a more potent, less irritating insect repellent.

Pregnant women might be particularly interested in such a breakthrough. Mosquitoes are attracted to carbon dioxide, and pregnant women exhale more carbon dioxide than the average person. Furthermore, a pregnant belly is a bit warmer than a normal belly, which may also appeal to mosquitoes.

Alcohol consumption has also been shown to increase the likelihood of bites. This may be because of a change in the blood's chemical makeup when it is processing a few drinks, and because of the rise in body temperature that comes with consuming too much alcohol.

Want to avoid mosquito bites? Stay away from alcohol, don't go outside if you are pregnant, and pray that you are among the lucky 15 percent of the population that doesn't secrete blood-type markers. If nothing else, hope others in your party have their neon lights flashing "Type O!"

ARE WE GOING TO BE HIT BY A METEOR?

We already have been, and we will be again. NASA estimates that about once every hundred years, a rocky asteroid or an iron meteorite big enough in size to cause tidal waves hits Earth's surface. About once every few hundred thousand years, an object strikes that is large enough to cause a global catastrophe.

NASA's Near Earth Objects program scans the skies and observes comets and asteroids that could potentially enter Earth's neighborhood. It has been keeping close tabs on an asteroid called Apophis, a.k.a. MN2004. According to NASA, on April 13, 2029, Apophis will be close enough to Earth that it will be visible to the naked eye. At one time, the odds were estimated to be as great as one in three hundred that Apophis would hit Earth. However, NASA has now ruled out a collision, which is a good thing because the asteroid would have hit Earth with the force of an 880-megaton explosion (more than fifty thousand times the power of the atomic bomb dropped on Hiroshima, Japan, in 1945).

Perhaps the best-known meteor hit occurred fifty thousand years ago, when an iron meteorite collided with what is now northern Arizona with a force estimated to be two thousand times greater than the bomb dropped on Hiroshima. Now named the Meteor Crater, the twelve-thousand-meters-wide crater is a popular tourist attraction.

A direct meteor hit isn't even necessary to cause significant damage. On June 30, 1908, what many believe was a small asteroid exploded high in the air near the Tunguska River in Russia. Taking into consideration the topography of the area, the health of the adjoining forest, and some new models concerning the dynamics of the explosion, scientists now believe that the force of the explosion was about three to five megatons. Trees were knocked down for hundreds of square miles.

NASA hopes to provide a few years' warning if there is a meteor approaching that could cause a global catastrophe. The organization anticipates that our existing technology would allow us to, among other things, set off nuclear fusion weapons near an object in order to deflect its trajectory. Or we can simply hope that Bruce Willis will save us, just like he did in the 1998 movie *Armageddon*.

WHY DOES AUSTRALIA HAVE SO MANY POISONOUS SNAKES?

Many people associate the cute and cuddly koala with Australia. And that's exactly the image the nation's tourism industry wants to tout: cute and cuddly. Deadly and dangerous wouldn't sell as many vacation packages, though it would be more accurate.

Australia is a place that would drive the snake-phobic Indiana Jones to the brink of insanity—there are snakes, snakes, and more snakes, many of which are poisonous. Of the approximately six hundred known venomous snakes in the world, a whopping sixty-one reside in Australia, according to the University of Sydney. And the Australia Venom Research Unit reports that eight of the ten most toxic land snakes on the planet are native to the continent.

Cute and cuddly? We think not. Thirty-five percent of the snake species in Australia are poisonous. Why does this continent host so many scary slitherers? Hundreds of millions of years ago, Australia was part of the supercontinent Gondwana, which also included South America, Africa, India, New Zealand, and Antarctica. Gondwana began to break up one hundred and fifty million years ago, and Australia snapped off altogether about fifty million years ago.

The snakes that were on the terrain now known as Australia included those from the Elapidae family, a group that had many venomous varieties. Once the Australian land mass broke off and became surrounded by water, the snakes had nowhere to go. So they developed new ways to survive on this biodiverse continent, which has a rain forest, vast deserts, and the largest coral reef on the planet. As is the case with natural selection, the strongest varieties lasted; many of today's venomous serpents are descendants of the Gondwana castaways.

Australia's venomous snakes come in a variety of lengths, colors, and attitudes, and they reside in many of the continent's environments. The deadliest—not just on Australia, but on the entire planet—is the inland taipan. This snake, part of the ancient Elapidae family, has venom potent enough to kill one hundred humans in a single bite. Close behind on the venom chart are the eastern brown snake and mainland tiger snake, which also hail from the dreaded Elapidae clan. Both can seriously ruin a vacation.

But don't let these snakes—or the continent's other poisonous critters, such as the box jellyfish or the funnel web spider—scare you away. If you visit Australia, the main predator you'll need to beware of is the human—specifically, those who are driving cars. Auto accidents cause more deaths each year in Australia than all of its poisonous creatures combined.

DID THE MARLBORO MAN DIE OF LUNG CANCER?

Yes—at least twice, in fact. There were, you see, many Marlboro men over the years. In 1954 Philip Morris hired the famous Leo Burnett advertising agency to revamp the Marlboro filtered cigarette brand, which the company had been marketing to women for thirty years. In light of magazine stories about the hazards of smoking, Philip Morris wanted to offer concerned male smokers the option of a "safe," filtered cigarette.

Leo Burnett launched a campaign featuring cowboys and other masculine figures, and before long Marlboro took off among men. In 1963–64, Philip Morris shifted the campaign exclusively to cowboys, who were usually portrayed by real cowboys. The Marlboro man in Marlboro country became one of the most recognized ad campaigns in history, and Marlboro became the nation's best-selling cigarette brand.

In the spring of 1992, former Marlboro model Wayne McLaren made waves when he announced that he was dying of brain cancer, which had started in his lungs. He told his story at the annual Philip Morris shareholders meeting and to the Massachusetts state legislature, which was considering a bill to increase taxes on cigarettes to fund health education. Soon after, McLaren made an anti-smoking ad, contrasting pictures of his rugged cowboy days with pictures of him near death in the hospital. He died the following June.

McLaren did not appear in many Marlboro ads, and Philip Morris initially claimed it had no knowledge that he had worked for the company. It later recanted, however, and admitted that McLaren had been featured in a series of promotional playing cards. But David McLean, a former Marlboro man who died from lung cancer in 1995, had appeared extensively in Marlboro TV and print ads in the 1960s. In 1996, his widow filed a high-profile lawsuit against Philip Morris and the major tobacco companies, claiming they were responsible for McLean's nicotine addiction that ultimately led to his death. The suit contended that McLean had to smoke up to five packs of cigarettes per take when shooting the Marlboro ads so that the photographers and videographers could get the pictures and footage they needed.

If you were to pick the Marlboro man out of a lineup, it probably would be Darrell Winfield, a former ranch hand who dominated Marlboro billboard and print ads in the 1970s and 1980s. When Winfield died in 2015, aged 85, no cause of death was listed in his obituary.

HOW LONG BEFORE YELLOWSTONE NATIONAL PARK EXPLODES?

And Which Way Should We Be Running?

About three million people visit the environs of Yellowstone National Park each year. They do a little hiking, maybe some fishing. They admire the majesty of the mountains and antagonize a few grizzly bears for the sake of an interesting picture. And, of course, they visit the geysers. Hordes of tourists sit and wait patiently for Old Faithful to do its thing every ninety minutes or so. When it finally blows, they break into applause as if they've just seen Carol Channing belt out "Hello, Dolly." And then they go home.

Few of these tourists give much thought to what is going on below their feet while they are at Yellowstone. Geologists, however, have known for years that some sort of volcanic activity is responsible for the park's strange, volatile, steamy landscape. Just one problem: they couldn't find evidence of an actual volcano, the familiar cone-shaped mountain that tells to us in no uncertain terms that a huge explosion once took place on that spot.

In the 1960s, NASA took the first pictures of the Yellowstone area from outer space. When geologists got their hands on these pictures, they understood why they couldn't spot the volcano— it was far too vast for them to see on the ground. The crater of the Yellowstone volcano includes practically the entire park, covering about 2.2 million acres. Obviously, we're not talking about your typical, garden-variety volcano. Yellowstone is what is known as a supervolcano.

There is no recorded history of any supervolcano eruptions, so we can only use normal volcanic activity as a measuring stick. Geologists believe that Yellowstone has erupted about 140 times in the past sixteen million years. The most recent blast was about one thousand times more powerful than the 1980 eruption of Mount St. Helens in Washington, and it spread ash over almost the entire area of the United States west of the Mississippi River. Some of the previous Yellowstone eruptions were many times more destructive than that. And here's some interesting news: in the past twenty years or so, geologists have detected significant activity in the molten rock and boiling water below Yellowstone. In other words, the surface is shifting.

Nearby, the Teton Range has gotten a little shorter. Scientists have calculated that Yellowstone erupts about every six hundred thousand years. And get this—the last Yellowstone eruption took place about 640,000 years ago.

Before you go scrambling for the Atlantic Ocean, screaming and waving your arms in the air, know that the friendly folks who run Yellowstone National Park assure us that an eruption is not likely to happen for at least another thousand years. And even then, any eruption would be preceded by weeks, months, or perhaps even years of telltale volcanic weirdness.

So don't worry. It's safe to go to Yellowstone. For now. But go easy on the bears, okay? Photography may be your favorite hobby, but theirs is mauling.

HOW MANY KIDS HAVE FOUND RAZOR BLADES IN THEIR CANDY APPLES?

It's Not All Fun and Games on Halloween

Halloween, All Hallows Eve, Samhain. Whatever you call it, October 31 is the night a kid's dreams come true. Not only do children get to dress up in fantastic costumes, but they also get to stand on their neighbors' porches and collect candy.

Parents are cautioned yearly to never allow their children to eat unwrapped candy that is collected on Halloween night. Whenever a child gets sick in early November and there's even the slightest chance that the illness is related to eating tainted candy, alarmists in the media call for parents to dump everything their children brought home. While these reports might be broadcast with the best of intentions—ensuring the safety of our children—almost all of them wind up being false alarms.

Sociologists refer to this as the "myth of the Halloween sadist." It's been causing yearly widespread panic since at least the 1970s, when a child died from an overdose of heroin that was said to have been given to him via Halloween candy. (This turned out to be untrue;

the heroin belonged to an uncle, and it was hidden away in the kid's Halloween loot by family members in an attempt to keep the uncle out of jail.) Since then, similar incidents have occurred, and in nearly every case, Halloween candy hasn't turned out to be the offender.

There have been more cases of foreign objects in Halloween goods than of tainted candy, especially since the late 1960s, and especially on the east coast. These reports usually involve pins, needles, or razor blades. New Jersey saw a rash of apples that did indeed have razor blades inserted into them—enough to warrant state legislative action on the topic—but few of the cases involved actual injury.

The most notable case of tampering occurred in 2000, when a man put needles in Snickers bars and handed them out to neighborhood children. No one, however, was seriously hurt.

The myth of dangerous candy persists today partly due to young pranksters. By taking candy that has been collected (say, your little brother's stash) and inserting something mildly dangerous, the prankster spooks an entire neighborhood and gets a good laugh. Urban legend debunker and sociologist Joel Best reports one such case, in which a child approached his parents with a candy bar that was sprinkled with ant poison.

The child, it turned out, did the sprinkling. It was good for a quick laugh, maybe, but these kinds of pranks perpetuate the notion that Halloween is a night for real parental fear.

IF ALL OF ACME'S PRODUCTS BACKFIRE, WHY DOES WILE E. COYOTE KEEP BUYING THEM?

Considering the number of failed ACME armaments and demolition devices that Wile E. Coyote employs in failed attempts to eradicate the Road Runner, we might conclude that ACME pays the clueless carnivore as a beta tester.

Wile E. Coyote has tried to catch his prospective prey using explosive tennis balls, earthquake pills, do-it-yourself tornado kits, jet-propelled pogo sticks, roller skis, instant icicle makers, and dehydrated boulders. Most of the damage he does is to himself, which makes sense—Wile E. Coyote is an addict.

That's right. In *Chuck Amuck: The Life and Times Of An Animated Cartoonist*, Wile E. Coyote creator Chuck Jones explains: "The Coyote could stop anytime—if he was not a fanatic. Of course he can't quit; he's certain that the next attempt is sure to succeed. He's the personality type that twelve-step programs are made for." Jones's thoughts are right in line with those of the late philosopher George Santayana, who said, "A fanatic is one who redoubles his effort when he has forgotten his aim."

If we want to be more charitable, we might view him as a symbol of the addictive personality. Jones's inspiration for the character came from Mark Twain's description in *Roughing It*. "The cayote [sic] is a living, breathing allegory of Want," Twain wrote. "He is always hungry. He is always poor, out of luck and friendless." Jones always thought of the coyote "as a sort of dissolute collie," he said in a 1989 *New York Times* interview.

So should Wile E. enroll in AA (ACME Anonymous, naturally)?
Probably not. As Jones says, "The Coyote is always more
humiliated than harmed by his failures." And the embarrassment
is never enough to keep him from trying yet another ACME
product. So don't quit now, Wile E. One of ACME's devices has
to work eventually—right?

HOW TERRIBLE WAS IVAN THE TERRIBLE?

About as cruel and terrible as anyone could be. It's pretty hard
to whitewash the reputation of a man who murdered friends,
tortured enemies, and beat his own son to death.

Ivan IV became ruler of Russia in 1533 at the tender age of
three, after his father died. His mother was a regent; her family
and other nobles—called boyars—fought each other often and
violently for control of the government. Ivan grew to hate them.
His tutors were monks, and he learned an intolerant brand of
Christianity that stayed with him his whole life.

In 1547, while still a teenager, Ivan had himself crowned the
first *tsar*—a word meaning "God's anointed." That's how
he thought of himself. He made pilgrimages, built churches,
and fancied himself chosen by God to hold absolute power—
including the power to kill anyone who disagreed with him.

In the early part of his reign, Ivan was not a bad ruler. He called
consultative assemblies, issued a new law code, reformed
local governments, and conquered some Tatar states. His first
marriage was happy and lasted more than twelve years. But

after his first wife died—he was married seven times—Ivan started behaving like a sadistic lunatic and earned his nickname, "the Terrible."

Convinced that his beloved wife had been poisoned by the hated boyars, Ivan attacked the people of that class by seizing their lands and executing them whenever he decided they were traitors. He also turned on old friends and advisors and had the highest-ranking church official in Moscow murdered. His most shocking crime was the murder of his own son and heir, Ivan, in 1581. He beat his adult son in front of the young man's wife, then delivered the death blow with an iron-pointed staff.

Ivan held onto power longer than any other Russian ruler. After Ivan died in 1584, his feeble-minded son, Feodor, took over because he was the infamous despot's last remaining heir. An autopsy done several centuries after his death revealed that Ivan's spine had been fused by disease, probably causing intense pain, which experts say may explain part of his insane behavior. But only part.

IF YOU LIVED IN SIBERIA AND TICKED OFF THE RUSSIAN GOVERNMENT, WHERE WOULD YOU BE SENT?

The frozen and desolate expanse of Siberia is infamous as a place of forced exile for Russian political dissidents. But if you already lived in Siberia and ran afoul of the authorities, where would you be sent? Possibly to a prison elsewhere in Russia, and anywhere would likely be better than Siberia.

Russia is the world's largest country by landmass, and Siberia accounts for more than 75 percent of the sprawling country— it's about 5.2 million square miles. Until very recently, large areas of Siberia were difficult to get to . . . and, thus, difficult to escape from. This made it an ideal place to send every politician, journalist, novelist, and poet who made difficulties for the Russian authorities. The Russian government started banishing people to distant parts of the country—not just Siberia—around the seventeenth century, and it continued to do so until after World War II.

Political and criminal exiles were sent to Siberian labor camps known as gulags. Many of these gulags were in extremely remote areas in northeast Siberia. Sevvostlag, a system of labor camps, was set up in the Kolyma region, within the Arctic Circle. Parts of the Kolyma mountain range weren't even discovered until 1926. It's a land of permafrost and tundra, with six-month-long winters during which the average temperature range is –2 degrees to –36 degrees Fahrenheit. Northeastern Siberia is home to the coldest town on the planet, Oymyakon, which once recorded a low of –96.2.

Siberia's first settlements were established relatively late in Russia's history, around the seventeenth century, but the region now supports several cities of more than half a million people. These are situated mostly in the south and have been accessible by rail since the early twentieth century. The storied Trans-Siberian Railway runs from Moscow east to Vladivostok, a distance of about 5,800 miles. The workforce that built the railway consisted of soldiers and, yes, labor-camp inmates.

DID CASTRATI SINGERS HAVE A CHOICE?

And If They Did, Who Would Say Yes?

This seems like a no-brainer. Ask a prepubescent boy if he wants to be castrated in order to keep his sweet, high falsetto voice. Would anyone say yes to that? Surprisingly, many did. In Italy, from before the seventeenth century and into the nineteenth century, approximately four thousand boys underwent castration, in the hopes that their preserved voices would make them sought-after singers. Since some of the boys were as young as seven, it was really their parents who gave consent. A boy of that age, even if he understood the operation, could hardly make an informed decision about it. So why did so many parents agree to this procedure? Fame and fortune—it's as simple as that.

The voices of castrati singers—male sopranos—were compared to the sounds of nightingales and angels. A gifted singer could amass great wealth performing for popes and kings. Composers like Mozart and Handel wrote pieces just for them. Castrati were popular with the ladies, too—they still had the major piece of equipment but couldn't make a woman pregnant.

Let's be clear on something: the point of the surgery was to preserve the voice. Castration in this context meant leaving the penis intact, and either removing the scrotum or cutting into the scrotum to sever the seminal vesicles. Once this was done, the boy's voice not only kept its high range, but the lack of testosterone also kept his vocal chords from hardening. His voice, then, was even more flexible than a woman's would be.

To many poor families, castration seemed a small price to pay for a chance at wealth, celebrity, travel, and the high life.

But why, you may wonder, did the choirs and opera companies need male sopranos? Why couldn't women be used to hit those high notes? Well, churches in those days still quoted a line from Saint Paul's epistle to the Corinthians, which said that women should be silent in church. So in Rome (where the Vatican is located) and in many—but not all—Italian cities, singers and choirs were exclusively male. As for theaters, where operas were staged—no decent woman would appear there.

But times changed. The gravy train ended for castrati singers in the nineteenth century. Napoleon and other rulers banned the operation; by 1870, even Italy had passed laws against it. Women had begun singing publicly, both onstage and in churches. The last castrato singer, Alessandro Moreschi, lived long enough to record his voice for posterity, in 1902, but he was far past his prime. His recording—which anyone can find on the Internet—does not come close to the soaring, beautiful tones that previous castrati had produced. Instead, it leaves you wondering what all the fuss was about.

ARE THERE ANY LEPERS LEFT?

And Should I Be Worried about Getting Leprosy?

Yes, there are about a quarter-million people worldwide with leprosy. It is found mostly in Southeast Asia and in the Third World countries of Africa and the Americas, although about a hundred cases are diagnosed in the United States each year. Cures for leprosy were developed in the 1960s and 1970s, and over the past fifty years, the number of afflicted has dropped from more than five million (perhaps as high as twenty million, according to some estimates) to the present figure.

For centuries, lepers were shunned: healthy men and women wouldn't so much as look at a leper because the grotesque disease was believed to be highly contagious. We now know that it's not—in fact, 95 percent of humans are naturally immune to it. Still, it's easy to see why the disease would have been so frightening. Leprosy starts with a small sore on the skin, which often goes numb as the disease begins to infect the peripheral nerves. If untreated, it can, in extreme cases, cripple and blind its victims.

This rarely happens today. Medicines as common as antibiotics are often effective at putting an end to leprosy. Patients can be cured of the disease in months or years, which has helped to erase much of the affliction's stigma. Doctors now avoid using the term "leprosy" because of its historically negative connotations and instead call it "Hansen's disease," after Norwegian doctor G. H. Armauer Hansen, who discovered the bacteria that causes it in 1873.

What about all of the awful stories relating to the disease? Most scientists think that the leprosy described in the Bible was a different sickness than the one that exists today. Hansen's disease does not turn the skin white, for example, so the leprosy of the Old Testament was probably a combination of several other ravaging infections, maybe even cancers.

Leper colonies really existed, from the Middle Ages through the twentieth century. Father Damien's famous leper colony in Hawaii and another colony in Carville, Louisiana, housed most of the unfortunate Americans who were diagnosed with Hansen's disease before treatments were developed, but there used to be many other centers around the world. Since the disease destroys the nerves and tissues of the body, it would have been horrifying to watch a victim succumb to it. Without a cure or a known cause, doctors thought it best to keep victims segregated from the healthy.

Doctors still aren't entirely sure how Hansen's disease is transmitted, though they suspect that the bacteria pass through the respiratory system. But since the treatments are so effective, and since most folks are immune, the search for an answer doesn't seem as pressing as it once did.

HOW MANY KIDS HAVE HAD AN EYE PUT OUT BY A BB GUN?

In any discussion of BB guns, anywhere in the civilized Western world (presumably), it's only a matter of time before someone brings up *A Christmas Story*. Ralphie, the movie's main character and BB gun afficionado, wants nothing on Earth so much as a Red Ryder, carbine action, two-hundred shot range air rifle. But every time he voices his desire, his mother has five words for him: "You'll shoot your eye out!" The line has become a mantra for concerned mothers—the classic BB gun block. When it comes to real kids in real backyards shooting real BB guns, how plausible is this concern?

Unfortunately for every ten-year-old who has ever petitioned his parents for one of these toy rifles, his mother's concern is somewhat justified. For example, according to a report filed by the Centers for Disease Control and Prevention, there were more than forty-seven thousand BB gun-related injuries to children and teenagers treated in emergency rooms across the country between June 1992 and May 1994. Of these, 2,839 (about 6 percent) involved an injury to the eye.

It's a rather small figure compared to injuries sustained to the arms, legs, hands, and feet, however; shots to the extremities comprised 54 percent of the reported injuries.

As famous as the mantra has become, shots to the eye are not the only ones to cause serious harm. There have been cases of BBs penetrating deep enough to become lodged in vital organs, and a report issued in 2004 quotes an average of four deaths a year due to BB guns and other non-powder rifles (those that fire by use of a spring, pressurized CO2, or pressurized air).

BB guns can be harmless toys when they're used properly, under the supervision of a mature adult, but their dangerous aspects should not be downplayed. Use of safety glasses and thick, protective clothing can reduce the possibility of injury, but teaching correct conduct and respect for guns (even when they only fire BBs) is the best way to avoid a trip to the local emergency room.

More than three million non-powder rifles are sold every year. Many are sold in department stores and toy stores, and many are sold to kids. Most states have no age restrictions when it comes to the sale of BB guns. If these kids are not taught to respect their guns, it may not be long before the toys are banned altogether. In fact, the state of New York has already done so.

"You'll shoot your eye out!" may be the easiest way to shoot down a ten-year-old's dream of owning a BB gun, but it's one of the least likely outcomes. Not every child with a BB gun is going to injure himself. And, in the event of an injury, it's much more likely that the BB will end up lodged in an extremity.

Maybe the mantra should be changed to, "You'll shoot your palm and end up with an unsightly metal ball trapped just below the skin for the rest of your life."

On second thought, we like the other phrase better.

WHY DOES HAIR GROW IN ALL THE WRONG PLACES WHEN YOU AGE?

The Older We Get, the Prettier We Ain't

In addition to the sagging, the wrinkles, the forgetting of car keys, excessive wind, and the spots of drooling, an ignominious side effect of aging is the dense thickets of hair that erupt from the ears, nose, and just about anywhere else you don't want them. While you have no choice but to accept the grim destiny of old age, you can at least know what cruel twist of anatomical fate produces this phenomenon.

Whether you are an incipient old man or old lady, the main culprit appears to be female hormones. And take notice of the word "appears." You should know up front that afflictions such as cancer and diabetes, not excessive nose hair, are what tend to get most of the medical attention and research funding. Consequently, the explanation that follows is mostly conjecture.

Both men and women produce female hormones such as estrogen. These hormones restrict the growth of body hair and counteract male-type hormones such as testosterone (which are also present in both men and women), which trigger the growth of body hair. When you're younger, the male and female hormones tend to maintain the balance they should. As you get older, production of the female hormones begins slowing down. In other words, the male–female hormonal balance gets out of whack, and you begin to look like a Yeti.

But it isn't all doom and gloom for hairy old-timers: they get cheap movie and museum tickets. General orneriness is allowed, or at least put up with. And they can force people to sit through their long, rambling stories.

WHY ARE COFFINS SIX FEET UNDER?

We've all heard the line in a cheesy movie that, against our better judgment, has sucked us in and stuck us to the couch: "One more move, and I'll put you six feet under." Whether the words are growled out by a cowboy in a black hat, an evil henchman, or a mobster in pinstripes, everyone knows what those six feet represent: the depth where coffins reside after burial. Or do they?

The bad guy may well mean what he says, but the final resting place for someone unfortunate enough to be in a coffin varies depending on the site of the funeral. Burial depths can range from eighteen inches to twelve feet. There's no world council that has decreed that a person must be put to rest exactly six feet under. Think about it. Digging a six-foot grave in a region below sea level, such as New Orleans, would get pretty soggy.

Most grave depths are determined by local, state, or national governments. New Orleans has dealt with its topographical issues by placing most of its dead above ground in crypts. The area's gravesites in the ground are almost always less than two feet deep—and even that doesn't prevent the occasional floater.

The California requirement is a mere eighteen inches. In Quebec, Canada, the law states that coffins "shall be deposited in a grave and covered with at least one meter of earth" (a little more than three feet). This is similar to New South Wales in Australia, which calls for nine hundred millimeters (slightly less than three feet). And the Institute of Cemetery and Crematorium Management in London says that "no body shall be buried in such a manner that any part of the coffin is less than three feet below the level of any ground adjoining the grave."

If burial depths vary from place to place, how did the phrase come to life? Historians believe it originated in England. London's Great Plague of 1665 killed over seventy-five thousand people. In Daniel Defoe's book *A Journal of the Plague Year*, he writes that the city's mayor issued an edict that graves had to be dug six feet deep to limit the spread of the plague outbreak. Other sources confirm Defoe's claim.

Of course, the plague is a scourge of the past, and today's world has no uniform burial depth. But who really cares? It still makes for a winning line in an otherwise schlocky movie.

IS CHIVALRY DEAD?

In fairy tales, chivalry is simple and straightforward. A man rescues his imprisoned princess, slays a dragon or two, and then takes the fair lady to the land of Happily Ever After. But in reality—specifically, present-day reality—the idea of chivalry is far more ambiguous.

Gallantry and courtesy are two traits embodied by the chivalrous man. He has to know how to open a door, pull out a chair, and protect the virtue of a woman. But herein lies the conundrum. Many modern American women pledge their allegiance to the ideal of independence, saying they don't need a man to take care of them; simultaneously, even a modern woman hopes the man who wins her heart will treat her like a princess.

The confusion dates back to the 1940s. World War II was raging, and women became the backbone of industry in the United States—they filled in at mills, factories, and foundries while the men fought overseas. By the 1950s, the war was over and women had returned to the home, resuming a subordinate role to men. All the while, though, changes were brewing, and they were actualized in the following decades:

The 1960s: Women's Lib took off, and bras were burned everywhere. Women wanted equal treatment in all walks of life; they refused to be treated like second-class citizens.

The 1970s: The Sexual Revolution was in full bloom. Women were the masters of their sexual destiny—sex was as free as speech.

The 1980s and Beyond: Women have made tremendous strides in areas once dominated by men. They now do far more than run homes—some run Fortune 500 corporations and hold high-ranking government positions. So is chivalry dead?

Not exactly. Like many issues facing men and women who are trying to cultivate a romance in these modern times, chivalry has become a source of confusion. Some men think that if a woman wants independence, she can open her own door and pay for her own meal. Some women, meanwhile, still like having that door opened and that meal paid for, even if they're perfectly capable of doing these things themselves.

A man who understands this duality—one who respects a woman's independence while still treating her with a sense of old-school decency—is seen as chivalrous in today's world. It might seem complicated, but frankly, it's a whole lot easier than slaying a dragon.

HOW DO BUGS KNOW YOU'RE ABOUT TO SQUISH THEM?

Nature's Mini-Ninjas

With some natural aptitude and years of training in an Eastern monastery, you may acquire certain fighting skills that let you drop a grown man to his knees in an instant—but even the most agile martial arts master struggles when it's time to swat a fly. Why? Insects may be tiny and powerless, but they have adaptations that give them an edge against the many larger forms of life that want to do them in.

For starters, the bugs that you most want to squish—flies, cockroaches, and the like—are equipped with compound eyes. A compound eye is a collection of structures called ommatidia. A fly, for example, has four thousand ommatidia in each eye; each ommatidium has its own light-sensing cells and a focusing lens that's positioned for a unique field of view.

Collectively, the elements of its compound eyes produce a panoramic vision of the bug's surroundings. The resolution of the resulting image isn't so hot, but it does the trick for detecting sudden movements from almost any direction.

Even when their supercharged vision fails them, insects have other ways to escape your wrath. Many bugs can actually feel the flyswatter approaching thanks to special sensory hairs called setae. When you start your bug-smashing motion, you push air between you and your target. This shift in air pressure stimulates the bug's setae, which signal the brain that something is coming. The movement of the setae gives the bug an idea of where the threat is coming from, and the bug reacts by scurrying in the opposite direction.

It also helps that some bugs are thinking about their getaways before it even seems necessary. In 2008, biologists at the California Institute of Technology used high-speed cameras to observe a group of flies. They found that it takes less than a tenth of a second for a fly to identify a potential threat, plan an escape route, and position its legs for optimal take-off.

In other words, when you're sneaking up on a fly and getting ready to strike, that fly has probably already spotted you and is prepared to zip away. This little bit of extra preparation helps pave the way for a Houdini-like escape.

Will the valuable information gleaned from this research enable us to finally gain the upper hand—quite literally—in our ongoing chess match against bugs? Don't count on it.

CAN YOU GET PARALYZED FROM THE WAIST UP?

For the average person, paralysis from the waist up would be truly disastrous. Not only would you look like you work for the Ministry of Silly Walks, but formerly simple acts like eating, talking, and even breathing would be impossible to accomplish on your own. Worst of all would be the TV situation. How would you operate the remote?

Before we can figure out whether this nightmare scenario is even possible, we need a refresher course on the human nervous system. The most central part of the nervous system is what we usually call—surprisingly enough—the central nervous system, which is made up of the brain and the spinal cord. The brain, of course, is where the action happens. Nerve impulses enter and your brain interprets them as sights, sounds, and sensations. Nerve impulses also exit—these are the commands your brain sends that put the parts of your body in motion. The other piece of your central nervous system, the spinal cord, serves as the conduit for all the signals as they enter and leave the brain.

Because the spinal cord is the link between the brain and the rest of the body, any damage to it is potentially disastrous. Injuries to the spinal cord are a leading cause of paralysis. Depending on what is injured, several types of paralysis are possible. Paraplegia—the most common condition, in which the legs are paralyzed—usually happens as a result of injuries to the lower part of the spine, which is known as the lumbar. A paraplegic retains command of his or her upper body because the nerves that serve those areas leave the spinal cord above the damaged area. But when the injury occurs higher on the spine, the arms and sometimes even the head are also affected; this condition is known as quadriplegia or tetraplegia.

So it may seem as if there is no way you can get paralyzed from the waist up—any damage to your spine that is up high enough to affect your arms will necessarily affect your lower extremities as well. But spinal injuries are not the only potential causes of paralysis.

Until now we've been talking mostly about the central nervous system—the brain and spinal cord. But once the nerves leave the spinal cord, they become part of what we usually call the peripheral nervous system, which is the fine network of nerves that is woven into the tissues of our body. Whenever you taste or touch or feel something, that nerve impulse begins in your peripheral nervous system. Likewise, when your brain sends a command to move the muscles of your body, it's the peripheral nervous system that executes the order.

Some illnesses—especially polio—can cause paralysis by damaging the peripheral nerves that trigger the muscles. Theoretically, an illness could strike only the nerves that affect the arms and torso, rendering a person paralyzed from the waist up. In fact, some cases of such a condition have been reported. Rarely, though, do these illnesses result in total paralysis from the waist up, nor is the paralysis usually permanent.

HOW DID MURPHY GET HIS OWN LAW?

Murphy's Law holds that if anything can go wrong, it will. Not surprisingly, the most widely circulated story about the origin of Murphy's Law involves a guy named Murphy.

In 1949, Captain Edward A. Murphy, an engineer at Edwards Air Force Base in California, was working on Project M3981. The objective was to determine the level of sudden deceleration a pilot could withstand in the event of a crash. It involved sending a dummy or a human subject (possibly also a dummy) on a high-speed sled ride that came to a sudden stop and measuring the effects.

George E. Nichols, a civilian engineer with Northrop Aircraft, was the manager of the project. Nichols compiled a list of "laws" that presented themselves during the course of the team's work. For example, Nichols's Fourth Law is, "Avoid any action with an unacceptable outcome."

These sled runs were repeated at ever-increasing speeds, often with Dr. John Paul Stapp, an Air Force officer, riding along in the passenger seat. After one otherwise-flawless run, Murphy discovered that one of his

technicians had mis-wired the sled's transducer, so no data had been recorded. Cursing his subordinate, Murphy remarked, "If there is any way to do it wrong, he'll find it." Nichols added this little gem to his list, dubbing it Murphy's Law.

Not long after, Stapp endured a run that subjected him to forty Gs of force during deceleration without any substantive injury. Prior to Project M3981, the established acceptable standard had been eighteen Gs, so the achievement merited a news conference. Asked how the project had maintained such an impeccable safety record, Stapp cited the team's belief in Murphy's Law and its efforts to circumvent it.

The law, which had been revised to its current language before the news conference, was quoted in a variety of aerospace articles and advertisements, and gradually found its way into the lexicon of the military and of pop culture.

It's important to note that "laws" that are remarkably similar to Murphy's—buttered bread always lands face down; anything that can go wrong at sea will go wrong, sooner or later— had been in circulation for at least a hundred years prior to Project M3981. But even if Edward Murphy didn't break new ground when he cursed a technician in 1949, it's his "law" we quote when things go wrong, and that's all right.

1. The longest coma on record lasted this long.
a. 42 years
b. 35 years
c. 9 years
d. 8 years

2. What is the record number of times a single person has survived being struck by lightning?
a. 7
b. 17
c. 3
d. 31

3. Which NFL team holds the record for most road games lost in a row (26)?
a. Detroit Lions
b. Cleveland Browns
c. Seattle Seahawks
d. Jacksonville Jaguars

4. Terry Lynn Nichols was sentenced to a record number of consecutive life sentences. How many?
a. 58
b. 161
c. 73
d. 211

5. Which of the following cities has the most cloudy days, on average?
a. Juneau, Alaska
b. Asheville, North Carolina
c. Hartford, Connecticut
d. Portland, Oregon

6. Which lake has the most radioactive contamination on the planet?
a. Onondaga Lake, United States
b. Lake Karachay, Russia
c. Zegrzenski Lake, Poland
d. Chao Lake, China

7. Which location gets the most rain per year?
a. Baton Rouge, Louisiana
b. Portland, Oregon
c. Lafayette, Louisiana
d. Hilo, Hawaii

8. The highest number of deaths to occur on Mount Everest in a single day is:
a. 209
b. 6
c. 43
d. 17

9. How many people did the worst fireworks accident on record kill?
a. 8
b. 80
c. 800
d. 8,000

10. Which of the following is the most contagious human disease?
a. Lyme disease
b. AIDS
c. Rotavirus
d. Tuberculosis

1.
a. 42 years

2.
a. 7

3.
a. Detroit Lions

4.
b. 161

5.
a. Juneau, Alaska

6.
b. Lake Karachay, Russia

7.
d. Hilo, Hawaii

8.
d. 17

9.
c. 800

10.
c. Rotavirus

ESPIONAGE

"THE FERRET HAS LOST THE MOLE—CALL THE EXTERMINATOR," SAID THE GARDENER TO THE MAILMAN

What's the best part of being a secret agent? The cool jargon? Advanced tech? Patriotic vindication? Those are occasional job perks, but there are downsides to the job. Occupational hazards include irregular hours, having to keep your story straight—oh, and you can get killed. But if you like breaking codes and messing with people's heads, this is a job that will keep your spooky mind engaged. Intelligence-gathering is an age-old pursuit, but the field has seen plenty of changes in the past two centuries, especially during major wars.

HOW WAS ENIGMA CRACKED?

Enigma was the code name for a portable cipher machine used by Germany to encrypt and decrypt messages. Invented in 1918 by a German engineer named Arthur Scherbius, the machine was initially marketed to businesses as a way of preventing corporate espionage. By 1933, the German Army, Navy, and Air Force were producing their own modified versions of the machine. With hundreds of millions of letter combinations, the German military thought their code was unbreakable.

How Did It Work?

Enigma encoded messages by performing sequential substitutions using electrical connections. The machine resembled a typewriter; it had 26 keys—one for each letter of the alphabet.

When a key was depressed, an electrical impulse traveled through a plug board at the front of the machine to a rotor contact inside the machine. The surface of each rotor also contained 26 electrical contacts, again representing letters of the alphabet. Each contact was wired to a key on the keyboard as well as to a contact on the next rotor. An output device illuminated the cipher letter the system created. The rotors were interchangeable, and extra rotors could be added. Enigma also used a device called a reflector, which redirected the electrical impulses back through the machine a second time. The code was exceedingly complex: Enigma could produce a combination of letters "so large that it has no name except 310114."

The Enigma was small enough to be carried into the field, but it required three men to operate: one typed the coded message into the machine, a second recorded the encrypted output one letter at a time, and a third transmitted the result in Morse Code.

Poland's Big Break

In 1932, Poland's intelligence corps received a package from its French counterparts containing Enigma guidelines that had been obtained by a German intelligence clerk named Hans-Thilo Schmidt. Schmidt was later arrested by the Nazis for the theft; he committed suicide in 1942 while in prison for treason.

Using some of Schmidt's information and a commercial version of the Enigma, three of Poland's brightest cryptanalysts successfully recreated the Enigma code and its indicator system in 1933. Though the commercial version was much different from the machines used by the German Army and Navy, Marian Rejewski, Henryk Zygalski, and Jerzy Rozycki deduced the internal wiring of Enigma's rotors. They used advanced mathematics, exploiting the German error of repeating the message setting (a three-letter sequence at the beginning of the transmission). The Poles developed two electromechanical machines that functioned similarly to the machines the Germans were using to decipher messages.

The Germans increased the sophistication of Enigma in 1939. By July of that year, Poland felt its independence threatened. The Polish Cipher Bureau gave its French and British counterparts all of its research in the hopes their teams could crack the new German code. The British had great success.

Britain's Best and Brightest

In 1939 the British intelligence community organized its code-breaking operations north of London at an estate called Bletchley Park. The British department operating out of the English manor was referred to as the Government Code and Cipher School.

The staff at Bletchley Park consisted of mathematicians, chess experts, linguists, computer scientists, and even a few crossword enthusiasts. They made several important discoveries, allowing them to break the Enigma code even when it was altered every two days. Their eventual success was due in part to German methods of coding:

• The reflector ensured that no letter could be coded as itself.
• Because the keyboard contained only letters, all numbers had to be spelled out.
• Military ranks, military terms, and weather reports appeared often, making it easier to decode these words.
• The Germans would not repeat rotor order within a month, and the rotors changed position every two days. This greatly reduced the combinations used in the machines by the end of the month, making it easier to crack those messages.

Allied forces eventually captured a few German U-boats and surface ships with intact Enigmas and codebooks, giving the code breakers the knowledge they needed to anticipate changes to the code. By 1943, most coded German communications were read routinely.

To Act, or Not to Act

Intelligence gleaned from decrypted Enigma messages fell under Ultra, the code name used by Britain, and later the United States. The codes of the Luftwaffe were the first broken by Britain's team of cryptologists, and Britain monitored the Luftwaffe traffic to learn of planned raids during the Battle of Britain. They also alerted Prime Minister Churchill to the fact that Germany wanted air superiority before launching an invasion of Britain. Messages intercepted between Rommel and Hitler revealed some of Rommel's planned tactics in Africa, giving the Allies an edge at Alam Halfa.

Cracking the Enigma was perhaps most useful to convoys crossing the Atlantic. As codes were broken and manuals captured, the Allies were able to locate and avoid U-boat patrols. While the breaking of the Enigma code did not win the war for the Allies, there can be no denying the feat shortened the war, saving many lives in the process.

DID THE UNION ARMY HAVE SPIES?

In a letter to President Lincoln dated April 21, 1861, private detective Allan Pinkerton offered his services and commented on one of the traits that would make him an icon of law enforcement for generations. "Secrecy is the great lever I propose to operate with," he wrote.

Born in Scotland in 1819, Pinkerton came to the United States in 1842. He originally was a barrel builder by trade, but his skills at observation and deduction led him to a career fighting crime. By age 30, he'd joined the sheriff's office of Cook County, Illinois, and been appointed Chicago's first detective. He later joined attorney Edward Rucker to form the North-Western Police Agency, forerunner of the Pinkerton Agency. As his corporate logo, Pinkerton chose an open eye, perhaps to demonstrate that his agents never slept. Clients began calling him "The Eye." Pinkerton and his operatives were hired to solve the growing number of train robberies, which became more and more of a problem as railroads expanded across the nation. George B. McClellan, president of the Ohio and Mississippi Railroad, took particular notice.

Wartime Duties

In 1861, Pinkerton's agency was hired to protect the Philadelphia, Wilmington, and Baltimore Railroad. In the course of their duties, Pinkerton and his agents learned of a pre-inaugural plot to kill President-elect Lincoln. The detectives secretly took Lincoln into Washington before he was scheduled to arrive, thwarting the conspirators. Lincoln was inaugurated without incident.

When the war began, Pinkerton was given the duty of protecting the president, becoming a forerunner of today's Secret Service. He was also put in charge of gathering intelligence for the army, now run by his old railroad boss, McClellan. The detective and his operatives infiltrated enemy lines. Using surveillance and undercover work, both new concepts at the time, agents gathered vital information. Pinkerton tried to get details any way he could. His people interviewed escaped slaves and tried to convince literate slaves to return to the South to spy. He used female spies, and he even infiltrated the Confederacy himself several times using the alias Major E. J. Allen.

Uncertain Information

While much of this was invaluable, his work was tarnished by a seeming inability to identify enemy troop strengths. His reports of enemy troops were detailed, including notes on morale, supplies, movements, and even descriptions of the buttons on uniforms. Yet the actual numbers of troops he provided were highly suspect.

In October 1861, as McClellan was preparing to fight, Pinkerton reported that Confederate General Joseph Johnston's troops in Virginia were "not less than 150,000 strong." In reality, there were probably fewer than 50,000. And the following year he reported the strength of Confederate General John Magruder at Yorktown, putting troop numbers at a whopping 120,000 when the true number was closer to 17,000. After the true strength of these forces was discovered, Pinkerton was ridiculed. Some historians believe that Pinkerton was unaware of the faulty information, but others insist he intentionally provided inflated figures to support McClellan's conservative battle plans. The truth will likely never be known, as all of Pinkerton's records of the war were lost in the Great Chicago Fire of 1871.

Return to Civilian Life

After McClellan, one of Pinkerton's staunchest supporters, was relieved of his command by Lincoln, Pinkerton limited his spying activities and shifted his work back toward criminal cases, which included the pursuit of war profiteers. He ultimately returned to Chicago and his agency, working there until his death in 1884.

DID DIXIE HAVE SPIES?

The Socialite Spy

Although she was already in her mid-40s by the time the Civil War erupted, Rose O'Neal Greenhow—a seductive Washington socialite and widow—used her wiles to keep Confederates informed of Northern movements.

Before the war, she had been known to entertain international diplomats and members of Congress, and she had been close to President James Buchanan. But when the South started to secede, her Southern sympathies prevailed, and soon she was enlisted to collect covert intelligence for the new Southern government. Befriending Colonel E. D. Keyes—who just happened to be the secretary to Union General-in-Chief Winfield Scott—Greenhow gained information that led directly to the Southern victory in the first major action of the war, the First Battle of Bull Run, in July 1861. For her efforts, officials in Richmond sent her a personal note of thanks.

In January 1862, Greenhow was arrested as a spy and, after a few months of house arrest, sent to Old Capitol Prison in Washington, D.C. Even from jail, however, she continued to collect Union secrets and pass them to the Confederates, hiding messages in a ball of yarn or a visitor's hair bun to transport the precious information.

Released in exchange for Union prisoners, Greenhow was exiled to the Confederacy and arrived in Richmond in June to a hero's welcome. Confederate President Davis personally received her party upon its arrival. But now that she was known in the North, her career as a spy in America was over. Davis sent Greenhow to Europe, where she sought political and financial support for the Confederacy.

In September 1864, Greenhow was returning to America aboard the blockade runner *Condor*. During a fierce storm, the *Condor* was pursued by a Union ship and ran aground. Greenhow tried to escape by rowboat but was thrown overboard. Weighed down by more than $2,000 in gold, Greenhow drowned. Her body later washed ashore, and she was buried with full military honors in Wilmington, North Carolina.

The Covert Chaplain

Thomas Nelson Conrad was one of the Confederacy's most colorful, ambitious, and effective spies. His initial plans included assassinating Union General-in-Chief Winfield Scott (whom he considered a traitor to his home state of Virginia) and kidnapping President Lincoln.

Prior to the war, Conrad had been headmaster at Georgetown College in Washington, D.C., but his enthusiasm for the South proved to be too much: he was arrested in June 1861 when he had "Dixie" played as the graduation's processional march. Upon his release, he signed up as a chaplain with General Jeb Stuart's Confederate troops in Virginia. As a man of the cloth, Conrad easily made his way into Union territory, where he was able to garner Union strategies and plans.

Conrad eventually returned to Washington, where he trimmed his hair and shaved his beard. The look made him a dead-ringer for John Wilkes Booth; in fact, Conrad was mistaken for Booth and briefly arrested for Lincoln's assassination.

Conrad returned to the academic world after the war, teaching first at Rockville Academy in Maryland and later at Virginia A & M, becoming president there in 1881. He recorded his adventures in his memoir, *The Rebel Scout*, and died in 1905.

A Confederate Charmer

As a courier for Rose O'Neal Greenhow, Antonia Ford held many parties for Union officers and soldiers at her home in Fairfax Court House, Virginia. Ever the socialite, she would charm her guests, who didn't realize she was collecting military information for the Confederates.

She became a favorite resource for General Stuart and was named an honorary aide-de-camp. She also provided Colonel John Mosby and his rangers with timely information that led to the kidnapping of Union General Edwin H. Stoughton in March 1863. Her luck couldn't last, however, and Ford accidentally blew her cover to a member of Pinkerton's Agency. She was arrested only days later.

A southern charmer to the end, Ford became romantically involved with her Union jailor, Major Joseph Willard, while staying in the Old Capitol Prison. He proposed, they married, and she signed a Union loyalty oath in 1864. Prison life had left its mark on Ford, however, leaving her sickly and weak. She died in 1871 at age 33.

The Squirrel Hill Spy

Laura Ratcliffe was also a valuable aide to Colonel John Mosby and his rangers, who often used her home in Squirrel Hill, Pennsylvania, for clandestine meetings. Ratcliffe allowed

Mosby to use a large rock there as a rendezvous where Confederates could exchange messages and keep money taken from Union plunder.

Ratcliffe was active in Confederate espionage throughout the war but was never caught. Later in life, she married a Union veteran named Milton Hanna. When she passed away in 1923, Ratcliffe's wake was set up in the front window of her house. Hundreds of people showed up to pay their last respects.

WHO WAS THE REAL "MAN WHO NEVER WAS"?

The rough tides slapped against the southern Spanish coast in the spring of 1943, carrying the mangled corpse of a British major who appeared to have drowned after his plane crashed into the sea. The body, one of thousands of military men who had met their end in the Mediterranean waters, floated atop a rubber life jacket as the current drifted toward Huelva, Spain. With a war raging in Tunisia across the sea, a drifting military corpse was not such an unusual event.

But this body was different, and it drew the immediate attention of Spanish authorities sympathetic to German and Italian Fascists. Chained to the corpse was a briefcase filled with dispatches from London to Allied Headquarters in North Africa concerning the upcoming Allied invasions of Sardinia and western Greece. The information was passed on to the Nazis, who accepted their apparent stroke of good luck, and now anticipated an Allied strike on the "soft underbelly of Europe." Unfortunately for them, the whole affair was a risky, carefully contrived hoax.

Rigging the "Trojan Horse"

Operation Mincemeat was conceived by British intelligence agents as a deception to convince the Italians and Germans that the target of the next Allied landings would be somewhere other than Sicily, the true target. To throw the Fascists and Nazis off the trail, British planners decided to find a suitable corpse—a middle-aged white male—put the corpse in the uniform of a military courier, and float the corpse and documents off the coast of Huelva, Spain, where a local Nazi agent was known to be on good terms with local police.

The idea of planting forged documents on a dead body was not new to the Allies. In August 1942, British agents planted a corpse clutching a fake map of minefields in a blown-up scout car. The map was picked up by German troops and made its way to Rommel's headquarters. He obligingly routed his panzers away from the "minefield" and into a region of soft sand, where they quickly bogged down.

This deception, however, would be much grander. If the planted documents made their way up the intelligence chain, Hitler and Mussolini would be expecting an invasion far from the Sicilian coast that Generals Eisenhower, Patton, and Montgomery had targeted for invasion in July 1943.

The Making of a Major

Operation Mincemeat, spearheaded by Lieutenant Commander Ewen Montagu, a British naval intelligence officer, and Charles Cholmondeley of Britain's MI5 intelligence service, found its "host" in early 1943 when a Welshman living in London committed suicide by taking rat poison. The substance conveniently produced a chemical pneumonia that could be mistaken for drowning.

The two operatives gave the deceased man a new, documented identity: "Major William Martin" of the Royal Marines. They literally kept the "major" on ice while arrangements for his new mission were made.

To keep Spanish authorities from conducting an autopsy—which would give away the body's protracted post-mortem condition—the agents decided to make "Major Martin" a Roman Catholic, giving him a silver cross and a St. Christopher medallion. They dressed the body, complete with Royal Marine uniform and trench coat, and gave him identity documents and personal letters (including a swimsuit photo of his "fiancée," an intelligence bureau secretary). With a chain used by bank couriers, they fixed the briefcase to his body.

Martin's documents were carefully prepared to show Allied invasions being planned for Sardinia and Greece (the latter bearing the code name Operation Husky). They also indicated that an Allied deception plan would try to convince Hitler that the invasion would take place in Sicily (the site of the real Operation Husky). With everything in order, the agents carefully placed the corpse into a sealed container—dry ice kept the body "fresh" for the ride out to sea.

The submarine HMS *Seraph* carried "Major Martin" on his final journey. On April 28, the *Seraph* left for the Andalusian coast, and two days later the body of a Royal Marine officer washed ashore. Within days, a set of photographs of the major's documents were on their way to Abwehr intelligence agents in Berlin.

Taking the Bait

Abwehr, Hitler, and the German High Command swallowed the story. After the war, British intelligence determined that Martin's documents had been carefully opened and resealed before being returned by the Spanish. The German General Staff, believing the papers to be genuine, had alerted units in the Mediterranean to be ready for an invasion of Sardinia and Greece. They moved one panzer division and air and naval assets off the Peloponnese, and disputed Italian fears of an impending invasion of Sicily.

The Allies captured Sicily in July and August 1943, and after the war, Commander Montagu wrote a bestselling account of Operation Mincemeat titled, *The Man Who Never Was*. The book was made into a film thriller a few years later.

Who was Major William Martin? The original body appears to have been a 34-year-old depressed Welsh alcoholic named Glyndwr Michael, and "Major Martin's" tombstone in Spain bears Michael's name. Historians have debated the identity of "Major Martin," however, theorizing that a "fresher" corpse from a sunken aircraft carrier was substituted closer to the launch date.

Whoever the real "Major Martin" may have been, one thing is certain: he saved thousands of lives, and became a war hero and action movie star in the process—quite an accomplishment for a dead man!

WHAT WAS THE FBI DOING DURING WORLD WAR II?

In the late 1930s, the Federal Bureau of Investigation (FBI) held the full confidence of the American public. Its G-men and their boss, the legendary J. Edgar Hoover, were looked on as heroes, and their tireless efforts to bring criminals to justice made them the subject of radio shows and even bubblegum cards. With the outbreak of the war in Europe, they were given an additional new responsibility: defending the United States against an enemy Hoover referred to as "international gangsters."

Enemies Within

In 1933, J. Edgar Hoover, head of the agency that would become the FBI two years later, was called on to investigate a death threat that had been made against Adolf Hitler. At the close of the 1930s, however, the United States was at least as interested in tracking the activities of the German leader as it was in his well-being.

In 1936, President Roosevelt asked Hoover to use his agency to produce a "broad picture" view of Fascist and Communist activities in the United States. Hoover, always extremely concerned with the possible existence of subversives, instructed his agency to proceed to gather information from "all possible sources." Those sources included covert means and illicit wiretaps, since this new function was not public knowledge. However, by 1939, the need for such secrecy disappeared when Roosevelt publicly announced that he was giving the Bureau the responsibility of handling cases of espionage, violation of neutrality laws, and sabotage.

With official sanction in place, the FBI began establishing the range of powers it would use throughout the war:

• The Bureau expanded its domestic surveillance program, asking telegram companies to delay sending messages until the FBI had time to make copies. Eventually the companies found it easier to simply make the copies themselves and hand them over to the agency.
• The Bureau hunted down draft dodgers.
• At least one agent trained in industrial security was placed in each field office to combat possible saboteurs.
• Special Intelligence Service divisions outside U.S. borders were set up to combat Axis activities in Latin America.
• Double agents were recruited to pass on false information to the country's adversaries for the length of the war.

The FBI also produced and monitored a list of potential Axis sympathizers: the Custodial Detention List. It put the list to use immediately after the attack on Pearl Harbor, overseeing the arrests of 3,846 people. Though his agency participated in those arrests, Hoover was against the more widespread internment of the Japanese-American populace that took place later, considering it an affront to the abilities of his Bureau. In his opinion the FBI had already identified all possible sources of danger, and further detentions were unnecessary.

Pastorius and Magpie

Paranoia about an enemy fifth column ran rampant in America, but it was not without basis, as two prominent incidents prove. In June 1942, Germany attempted to strike at America's home front in an action called Operation Pastorius. The Nazi intelligence service had recruited eight English-speaking men who were trained in explosives, chemistry, secret writing, and how to blend into American surroundings. One had even served in the U.S. military. The men were given thousands of dollars, some of which was for bribes, and instructions to destroy targets ranging from power plants to Jewish-owned businesses.

They entered the country via U-boats off the coasts of Amagansett, Long Island and Ponte Vedra Beach, Florida, intent on creating havoc. The plot began to unravel when the Coast Guard found traces of the Long Island landing and alerted the FBI. Finally, one of the saboteurs turned himself in to the FBI, leading to the capture of the other seven.

A second operation, code-named Magpie, took place in November 1944 when Germany landed two agents in Maine. The men were charged with observing the 1944 presidential election as well as obtaining any technical information they could find on rocketry or nuclear research. The men were spotted and reported to the FBI by at least two people, one a Boy Scout living up to his promise to do his duty to his country. Again, one of the conspirators turned himself in to the FBI, and the operation was quickly shut down.

The agency made the most of these events from a public relations point of view. The Bureau downplayed the saboteur who turned himself in, and instead gave the public an image of an agency inexorably hunting down Axis spies. Despite the blatant public-relations maneuvering, there was legitimate cause for pride. The FBI left the war years much stronger than it had entered them, having increased its workforce from 700 to 12,000 people in a decade, and the U.S. home front was largely safe from serious attacks during the war.

WERE THERE FEMALE ESPIONAGE AGENTS IN WWII?

In Europe in the 1940s, the "invisibility" of women often made them ideal operatives. They could eavesdrop in public or witness encounters with authorities unnoticed. Britain's Special Operations Executive (SOE) realized that female agents could be especially effective in the field.

Hedgehog

When France fell in 1940, Marie-Madeleine Fourcade helped establish a partisan resistance group called Alliance. Headquartered in Vichy, the group became known as "Noah's Ark" after Fourcade gave its members names of animals as their code names. Her own code name was "Hedgehog." The group worked to obtain information about the German armed forces and passed the intelligence on to the SOE. The Alliance was among the first partisan groups organized with the help of the SOE, which supplied the French operatives with shortwave radios and millions of francs dropped by parachute.

Although Fourcade was one of the Alliance's top agents, she was caught four times by the Germans; she escaped or was released each time. Once she was smuggled out of the country in a mailbag. On another occasion, she escaped from prison by squeezing through the bars on the window of her prison cell.

While Fourcade's luck held, other members of Noah's Ark were captured in 1944 during a botched partisan operation aiding the Allied advance in Alsace. They were later executed at the Natzweiler-Struthof concentration camp in France. Fourcade managed to survive the war and wrote a book about her experiences, *Noah's Ark*, published in 1968. She died in a military hospital in Paris in 1989 at age 79.

Louise

Born to a French mother and an English father, Violette Bushell Szabo joined SOE after her husband, a Hungarian serving in the Free French Army, was killed at the Battle of El Alamein. She was given the code name "Louise." Following intensive espionage training, Szabo parachuted into France near Cherbourg on April 5, 1944. On her first mission, she studied the effectiveness of resistance, and subsequently reorganized a resistance network that had been destroyed by the Nazis.

She led the group in sabotage raids and radioed reports to the SOE specifying the locations of local factories important to the German war effort. Szabo returned to France on June 7 and immediately coordinated partisans to sabotage communication lines. The Germans captured her three days later, reportedly after she put up fierce resistance with her Sten gun.

Szabo was tortured by the SS and sent to Ravensbrück concentration camp, where she was executed on February 5, 1945 at age 23. Three other female members of the SOE were also executed at Ravensbrück: Denise Bloch, Cecily Lefort, and Lilian Rolfe. Szabo became the second woman to be awarded the George Cross (posthumously) and was awarded the Croix de Guerre in 1947.

Palmach Paratroops

Haviva Reik and Hannah Senesh were Eastern European Jews who joined the SOE to help liberate their homelands. Reik was born in Slovakia and grew up in the Carpathian Mountains. Senesh, a poet and playwright, was born in Budapest. The daughter of a well-known playwright and journalist, she enjoyed a comfortable, secular life before discovering Judaism as a teenager. Both women immigrated to Palestine in 1939 and joined the Palmach, a paramilitary branch of the Zionist Haganah underground organization. Trained as parachutists, Reik and Senesh were 2 of more than 30 Palestinian Jews dropped behind German lines on secret SOE missions.

In March 1944, Senesh parachuted into Yugoslavia and, with the aid of local partisans, entered Hungary. She was almost immediately identified by an informer and arrested by the Gestapo. "Her behavior before members of the Gestapo and SS was quite remarkable," an eyewitness later wrote. "She constantly stood up to them, warning them plainly of the bitter fate they would suffer after their defeat." Though brutally tortured, she refused to give up her radio codes. On November 8, she was executed by a firing squad. "Continue the struggle till the end, until the day of liberty comes, the day of victory for our people," were her final written words.

In September 1944, Reik and four other agents parachuted into Slovakia to provide aid for an uprising against the Fascist puppet government, and assist the Jews in the passage to Palestine. Back in her native Banska-Bystrica, she aided refugees, helped Jewish children escape to Palestine, and joined resistance groups in rescuing POWs. In October, Nazis occupied the town. A few days later, Haviva and her comrades were captured in their mountain hideout by Ukrainian Waffen-SS troops. On November 20, they were executed. The remains of Reik, Senesh, and five other SOE agents were buried in Israel in 1952, in the Israeli National Military Cemetery in Jerusalem.

WHO WAS "DIANE"?

"We Must Find and Destroy Her!"

During stints for both British and U.S. intelligence, Virginia Hall so excelled at her duties that she became a marked woman by the Gestapo and ultimately was awarded the U.S. Distinguished Service Cross. "The woman who limps is one of the most dangerous Allied agents in France," proclaimed Gestapo wanted posters, showing a young brunette American. "We must find and destroy her." So dangerous was Virginia Hall's position that even her wooden leg was given a code name, "Cuthbert." Escaping France by crossing the Pyrenees on foot in November 1942, Hall cabled London that "Cuthbert is giving me trouble, but I can cope." Misunderstanding that Cuthbert was another agent, a Special Operations Executive (SOE) officer cabled back, "If Cuthbert is giving you trouble have him eliminated."

Born in Baltimore, educated at Radcliffe and Barnard colleges, and fluent in French and German, Hall had aspired to a Foreign Service career and worked at the U.S. Embassy in Warsaw in 1931. Her hopes were dashed a year later when she accidentally shot herself during a hunting trip in Turkey and her left leg was amputated. In Paris at the outbreak of World War II, Hall volunteered for the French Ambulance Service Unit. When France fell to Germans in June 1940, Hall trekked to London and volunteered for British intelligence.

During 15 months of SOE service, Hall was instrumental in Britain's effort to aid the French resistance. Working from Vichy, she posed as an American journalist while securing safe houses, setting up parachute drop zones, and helping rescue downed Allied airmen. After the United States entered the war, Hall went underground. Her position became untenable when German troops occupied Vichy following Rommel's defeat in North Africa and she barely escaped to Spain.

Back in Britain, Hall volunteered for the U.S. Office of Strategic Services (OSS) and trained in Morse code and wireless radio operation. Unable to parachute because of her leg, she landed in Brittany by British patrol boat prior to the D-Day invasion. Code-named "Diane," she contacted the French Resistance in central France and helped prepare attacks supporting the Normandy landings.

Still hunted by the Gestapo, Hall adopted an elaborate disguise as a French milkmaid, layering her fit physique with heavy woolen skirts that hid her limp. Peddling goat cheese in city markets, she listened in on the conversations of German soldiers to learn the disposition of their units. Hall helped train three battalions of partisan fighters that waged a guerrilla campaign against the Germans and continued sending a valuable stream of intelligence until Allied troops reached her position in September 1944.

After the war, President Truman awarded Hall the Distinguished Service Cross, though she turned down a public presentation to protect her cover for future intelligence assignments. In 1951, she joined the CIA as an intelligence analyst and retired in 1966. She died in Rockville, Maryland, in 1982.

HOW DO YOU BECOME A PRIVATE EYE?

The first private eye on record was a French criminal and privateer named Eugene Francois Vidocq, who founded a private investigation firm in 1833. Vidocq was hardly a man with a spotless record, and neither were his employees: most of his investigators were his friends who were ex-convicts and other citizens of questionable character. Vidocq was periodically arrested by the police on a series of trumped-up charges, but he was always released after they failed to produce enough evidence. Despite his background, Vidocq made significant contributions to the field of investigation, including record keeping, ballistics, indelible ink, and unalterable bond paper.

The Modern PI

Fast forward to recent statistics from the U.S. Department of Labor, which state that in 2006, there were approximately 52,000 working gumshoes. While more than a third of working private investigators have college degrees, many have only high school diplomas or Associate degrees, and some have neither. Those with college degrees come from varied backgrounds, such as accounting, computer science, business administration, or the dozens of other majors whose curriculum lends itself to specific types of investigative work. Interestingly, most private investigators do not have a degree in criminal justice.

Talk to anyone who's knowledgeable about the business and they'll tell you that the prerequisites for success are a thirst for answers and the ability to root out details after everyone else has come up empty handed. Superior communication skills and a special area of expertise, say, in computers, also come in handy. The most successful private eyes are people who can think logically, apply their unique knowledge to a problem, and consistently come up with creative means to their ends.

A Day in the Life

Depending on their background, private investigators can work for a variety of employers: individuals, professional investigative firms, law firms, department stores, or bail bondsmen. One place they can count on *never* working is for the local police department or the FBI. Government agencies rarely interface with private firms. Unfortunately, that nixes the dramatic image of a lone-wolf PI getting a call in the middle of the night because the police are stumped. The majority of cases have to do with locating lost or stolen property, proving that a spouse has been unfaithful, finding missing friends or relatives, conducting background investigations, or proving that a business associate absconded with the company cash.

Much of the work that private investigators do involves long hours sitting behind the wheel of a car doing surveillance. Only the highest- profile cases involving investigative firms with large operating budgets can afford sophisticated surveillance vans loaded with high-tech equipment. Other cases require collecting facts the old- fashioned way—interviewing suspects and witnesses in person. Facts that can't be collected that way are often obtained by perusing public records by computer, or researching tax records, business licenses, DMV records, real estate transactions, court records, and voter registrations.

But how much can a private eye expect to make? Fortunately, the entertainment industry has painted a rather broad picture of the private investigation business. For every television show about a PI living on a Hawaiian estate, there's another show about a PI living in a dilapidated trailer house on the beach.

The truth is, the median salary for private investigators in May 2006 was $33,750. The middle 50 percent earned between $24,180 and $47,740; the lowest and highest 10 percent earned $19,720 and $64,380, respectively. Not too shabby, but probably not the lap of luxury, either.

Still Want to Be a Private Eye?

For those who remain undaunted by the proposition of drinking their dinner out of a thermos and spending ten hours a day in a car or cubicle for $25,000 a year, here's some insight on how to pursue a career in private investigation: many private investigators have retired early from military, police, or fire department careers. Having pensions or retirement funds can help with "getting over the hump" until the earnings as a PI increase. Some states require specific schooling while others require new investigators to spend time completing on-the-job training before applying for their license. Most states have licensing requirements for becoming a PI, so it's important to look into what's required and how long it takes before one can expect to begin to make a decent living. If the type of work requires that private investigators carry a firearm, a private eye will need to look into the local ordinances for carrying a concealed weapon.

If nothing else, private investigation can certainly be a fascinating and challenging career choice that promises a break from the ordinary job doldrums. So grab that Beretta, rev up that Ferrari, and get ready for your new life as a gumshoe!

1. What is a brush contact?
a. A botched surveillance activity
b. A brief public meeting between two spies
c. An act that inadvertently destroys evidence
d. A planned act of arson

2. What does the L in L-pill stand for?
a. Luminal
b. Lethal
c. Love
d. Location

3. Camp Swampy is the nickname for what?
a. A covert CIA training base
b. A place where opposing agents can parley
c. An agent's temporary field headquarters
d. Compromised information

4. What is a black bag job?
a. Planting explosives on an enemy
b. Planting incriminating evidence on an enemy
c. The creation of a code language
d. Covert entry into a building for surveillance purposes

5. Catching a leak by giving different versions of sensitive information to each suspected leaker is called:
a. A canary trap
b. A dinner bell
c. Shake them and bake them
d. A closet ploy

6. In CIA terminology, sheep dipping means:
a. Disguising agent identities by placing them in legitimate organizations
b. Brainwashing agents into believing their own cover stories
c. Getting rid of evidence
d. Giving marked money to suspected criminals

7. A spy's "window dressing" may refer to:
a. Their form of transportation
b. Their weapon
c. Their real political affiliation
d. Their cover story

8. An agent who pretends to be interested in defecting to another intelligence group is called:
a. A jackrabbit
b. A duplicant
c. A dangle
d. A mole

9. This slang term refers to the headquarters of an espionage service.
a. The hotel
b. Up the creek
c. Under the bridge
d. Uncle

10. A trap that uses sex to lure an enemy agent into disclosing classified information is called:
a. A beehive
b. A honeypot
c. A mousetrap
d. A flytrap

1.
b. A brief public meeting between two spies

2.
b. Lethal

3.
a. A covert CIA training base

4.
d. Covert entry into a building for surveillance purposes

5.
a. A canary trap

6.
a. Disguising agent identities by placing them in
   legitimate organizations

7.
d. Their cover story

8.
c. A dangle

9.
d. Uncle

10.
b. A honeypot

GAMES AND SPORT

IS THIS JUST A GAME TO YOU?

Children play games. Adults who should be working play games. All kinds of animals play games. What is it with all the game playing on this planet? Life is serious. Get back to work.

Actually, there's a very good reason for it. Ever heard of Play Theory? It's a real thing. Humans (and other mammals) develop important, real-world skills via play. For us, this can include language and logic skills, creativity, social competence, and motor skills. So go ahead—put on your silver cape and helmet and vroom around the office a couple times. You have skills to develop.

HOW DID CROSSWORD PUZZLES GET STARTED?

They debuted as "word-cross" puzzles in December 1913. Arthur Wynne invented the first batch, which had no black squares. Three weeks after the first puzzle appeared in the *New York World*, a typesetter accidentally reversed the name, and "word-cross" became "cross word." Everyone liked the change.

Wynne edited the "Fun" section of the *New York World*. Born in Liverpool in 1862, he emigrated to the United States in 1905 and retired from the newspaper business five years after inventing the crossword puzzle. The *New York World* newspaper folded in 1931, and Wynne died in 1945. End of story? Not quite.

Wynne's contribution to American culture became a phenomenon. Dozens of newspapers constructed and ran their own weekly puzzles. By the early 1920s, crosswords were popular in Great Britain, Germany, France, and Russia.

In 1924, two New York entrepreneurs saw an opportunity. The story is that Richard Simon's aunt loved crossword puzzles and asked her nephew to find her a book of them. He couldn't, so he formed a company with partner Max Schuster and published the first crossword puzzle book. They printed 3,600 books on the first go-round, and America went crossword crazy. Simon & Schuster reprinted and sold more than a quarter-million copies in the first year, and their upstart company is now one of the largest publishing houses in the world.

WHAT ARE SOME OTHER GREAT WORD GAMES?

To solve crosswords, a knowledge of trivia is helpful, but the talent of recognizing words from just a few of their letters is equally useful. That skill is useful in many word games as well, such as the classic *Ghost*, which can be played by any number of people. One person chooses a letter (let's say *p*). The next person adds a letter after it (say, *h*, bringing us to PH). Play continues in turn, with each person adding a letter while trying to avoid completing a word. PH might become PHA, then PHAN, then PHANT, then PHANTA. At that point someone might challenge, thinking that PHANTOM was the only possible word under construction (it's illegal to make a play without having a real word in mind—though you can get away with it if no one challenges you). This one would be a fruitless challenge, though, if the player had PHANTASMAGORICAL in mind . . . though another player would haplessly lose by the time they got to the m, since PHANTASM is also a word. In *Super Ghost*, a variant of the game, letters can be added before or after the existing set of letters, so the string PHANT could also end up as ELEPHANTINE.

Another fun word game is called *Dictionary Game*. If you've ever played the board game *Balderdash*, you're probably familiar with the conceit of this game. One person is chosen to get the game started, and he or she will flip through the dictionary looking for an obscure and unusual word. The player's goal is to select a little-known word that no one will recognize. Each player writes down the word and then thinks of a definition for it—hopefully one that will seem convincing— writes it down, and passes their paper to the leader. Meanwhile, the leader writes down the word and the correct definition. Once everyone has turned in their answer, the leader reads all the definitions out loud (including the real one). Each player guesses which one they think is the real definition. Players get a point for guessing correctly. If they happen to know the correct definition and write it down, they get three points. If no one guesses correctly, the leader gets a point. Play until each person has had a chance to choose a word from the dictionary. After everyone has had a turn, the player with the most points wins.

HOW CAN YOU EXERCISE YOUR BRAIN?

Looking to roll back the cognitive clock? Or maybe just remember where you put your car keys? Cognitive "training"— that is, doing mentally challenging activities such as crossword puzzles and sudoku—has been all the rage for a while because it's been shown to help preserve brain function. But there's another kind of workout that could be the real ticket to keeping your brain young.

Stay Sharp and in Shape

Studies show that regular, moderate exercise helps our brains stay sharp. Researchers have found that one hour of aerobic exercise three times a week can increase brain volume, which in turn may delay some age-related changes. It takes only a few months to start seeing results, suggesting that it's never too late to start exercising. Other studies done on animals concur that more exercise equals better brain function. Even the dormant neural stem cells in elderly mice "wake up" once the critters hit the running wheel.

In one study that examined older men and women with memory problems, mental workouts (in the form of brain teasers and puzzles) produced encouraging results when combined with physical exercise and a heart-healthy diet. What's good for the cardiovascular system appears to also be good for our gray matter, giving us another reason to lower our blood pressure, weight, and cholesterol levels.

Experts caution not to waste money on dietary supplements and vitamins that claim to have "anti-aging" benefits, and we don't need to buy special "brain fitness" computer programs. Engaging in a pleasurable activity, such as studying a foreign language, reading, or playing a musical instrument, is a great way to keep us thinking and learning.

WHAT'S UP WITH PINBALL?

Pinball was invented in the 1930s, inspired by the 19th-century game bagatelle, which involved a billiards cue and a playing field full of holes. Some early pinball arcades "awarded" players for high scores, and in the mid-1930s, machines were introduced that provided direct monetary payouts. These games quickly earned pinball the reputation as a fun diversion—and a gambling device. Thus, starting in the 1940s, New York City Mayor Fiorello LaGuardia declared pinball parlors akin to casinos ("magnets for the wrong element"), ushering in an era of pinball prohibition. Chicago, Los Angeles, and other major American cities followed suit with their own pinball bans. New York's pinball embargo lasted until 1976, and city officials destroyed 11,000 machines before it was lifted. The turning point: writer and pinball wizard Roger Sharpe called his shots during a demonstration in front of the New York City Council, proving that pinball was indeed a game of skill. The council members voted 6–0 to legalize pinball in the Big Apple.

Rise and Fall

Despite the fact that pinball was banned in the three largest U.S. cities, it became a favorite pastime among adolescents and teens in the 1950s. This changed in 1973 with the advent of the video game, but pinball enjoyed the first of several revivals later in the 1970s, thanks to its association with such rock-and-roll luminaries as The Who, Elton John, and Kiss. The last pinball renaissance peaked with Bally's *The Addams Family* game, introduced in 1991 to tie in with the release of the movie. It became the best-selling pinball game of all time, with 22,000 machines sold. In the 1990s, the bottom dropped out of the pinball market. By 2007, there was only one American manufacturer, Stern Pinball. A few boutique companies have appeared since then, but the market remains grim.

Origin of the Flippers

Gottlieb's Humpty Dumpty, designed by Harry Mabs in 1947, was the first pinball game to feature flippers (three on each side) that allowed the player to use hand-eye coordination to influence gravity and chance. Many pre-flipper games were essentially dressed-up gambling contraptions, and players could just tilt the machines to rack up points. Humpty Dumpty and the thousands of flipper games that followed were true contests of skill. In 1948, pinball designer Steven Kordek repositioned the flippers (just two) at the bottom of the playfield, and the adjustment became the industry standard.

HOW CAN I ROB VEGAS BLIND?

After all, most people would if they could. Few bother to try. We asked some questions about the fine art of betting, and its shady side. Here's what we found out.

How Would Someone Mark Cards?

You need two things: very sharp eyes and a deck with a repeating pattern on the back—Bicycles, Bees, and Aviators are great, but corporate logo decks are terrible. Ideally, use cards with backs printed in a color matching a fine-tip permanent marker. Then decide what mark will encode each suit and rank, and very carefully mark the cards. Since cards can be upside-down, and since most people fan them so as to view the upper left corners, mark both the upper left and lower right of each card. Wear prescription sunglasses so people can't see you staring at the backs of the cards they're holding.

Does Card Counting Really Work in Blackjack?

That depends on how many decks there are, first of all. The more decks are used at once, the less fruit card counting can bear. There are two types of card counting: in your head and mechanically assisted. The casino can't stop you from counting cards in your head; it can only make it more difficult for you. Some states have laws against mechanical assistance, and if you're caught with it, expect a quick blackball from every casino in the region.

Is Anyone Getting Away with Counting Cards?

Have no doubt of that. You'll never hear of them, because they will never be caught. Pigs get fat; hogs get slaughtered, as tax accountants say. They make reasonable money, they go to different places, they lose sometimes, they act like your everyday gambling addict or hobbyist. They don't give the game away by placing suspicious bets; they know how to behave, be friendly, flirt with employees. They stay under the radar. When the numbers are in their favor, they bet more; when numbers aren't good, they bet less, but they don't overdo it.

How Do Casinos Battle Card Counters?

First of all, from the pit boss to the security office, people are watching. When gambling, you should consider yourself under surveillance from head to toe. I wouldn't put it past casinos to have night-vision cameras underneath the tables. They have a lot of experience and know what to look for.

Free drinks are another tool, because hardly anyone's counting skills improve with alcohol intake. If the boss thinks you're counting, he or she may "flat bet" you—ask you to make the same wager on every hand, which is the opposite of what a counter is trying to do. What they're looking for is your reaction to that request. If you don't follow it, they'll ask you to leave.

What Are the Best and Worst Games in Terms of Payout?

Casino poker, blackjack card counting, and video poker generally pay best. Slot machines are terrible, as are live keno and Wheel of Fortune. House payouts tend to range from 85 to

95 percent overall, so on the whole, the game favors the casino. Do you think all those pyramids, sphinxes, complimentary buffets, and neon lights come from the money people have won?

WHY DO MOST SPORTS GO COUNTERCLOCKWISE?

For most non-athletes living their quiet day-to-day lives, doing things clockwise seems pretty intuitive. Doorknobs turn clockwise, screws are tightened clockwise, and yes, clocks run clockwise. Board games usually move clockwise, blackjack dealers hand out cards clockwise, and people in restaurants usually take turns ordering in a clockwise direction.

Yet in many of our sports, such as baseball and all types of racing, play moves in a counterclockwise direction. This can cause some serious confusion for clockwise-oriented individuals—just ask any T-ball coach trying to shepherd a young hitter down the first-base line.

How did this counterintuitive situation come to be? Part of the answer is rooted deep in history, of course. In ancient times, when the Roman Empire ruled virtually the entire known Western world, a popular form of entertainment was chariot racing. As Charlton Heston fans know, chariot racing moved in a counterclockwise direction.

Roman horses were invaluable in war and were trained to turn to the left to give right-handed spear-wielding riders an advantage in battle; in the Circus Maximus, it was natural to build the track to suit this. Considering the power of habit in human social development, it seems reasonable to assume that future forms of racing simply adopted the same direction of travel as the mighty Romans.

Some science-minded individuals logically postulate that foot racing goes counterclockwise due to physical forces. Because most people are right-handed (and right-footed), a counterclockwise motion tends to help those with a dominant right leg speed around turns. This is because of centrifugal force, which we're sure everybody remembers from high school physics. For those who have forgotten (or slept through physics class), centrifugal force is that sense of momentum— called inertia—that tries to keep you going in a straight line when you're trying to turn. A right-legged individual moving counterclockwise, this explanation contends, will have a better chance of counteracting this force.

Some sports move the other way. In England, for example, horse races travel in a clockwise direction. This seems particularly baffling, considering that American horse racing—which was brought over by the British during colonial times-—moves counterclockwise. It turns out, though, that counterclockwise horse racing actually developed in the United States in response to the British tradition.

One of the very first American horse tracks built after the Revolutionary War was established in 1780 by patriotic Kentuckian William Whitley. Flush with pride at the newly won independence of the colonies, Whitley declared that horse racing in the new country should go in the opposite direction of those stodgy, tyrannical Brits.

Baseball, in which runners move counterclockwise around the bases, also may have descended from a British ancestor. Some baseball historians have postulated that the modern national pastime may be based on a British bat-and-ball game called rounders. Interestingly, rounders players moved in a clockwise direction around the bases; why this was reversed in the rules of baseball is not known.

Possibly, the counterclockwise movement has to do with the orientation of the diamond. It's far easier for right-handers to throw across the diamond to first base if the runner is moving in a counterclockwise direction (which is also why you almost never see lefthanders playing any infield positions except for first base).

Of course, from one perspective, clockwise and counterclockwise are meaningless terms. Some physicists enjoy pointing out (somewhat smugly, we might add) that direction is entirely relative. Which means that those seemingly confused T-ball toddlers might be a lot smarter than we think.

HOW DO BOOKIES SET ODDS ON SPORTING EVENTS?

To answer this question, we need to learn a little about the sports book biz. Consider this gambling primer: bookies take a small percentage of every bet that comes in; this is known as the *vig*. The ideal situation for any bookie is to have an equal amount of money riding on both sides of a bet; this way, no matter what happens in the game, the bookie will make money. The bookie will pay out money to those who bet on the winner, take in money from those who bet on the loser, and come out ahead because of the vig. If everyone bets on one team and that team wins, the bookie will lose a lot of money. Sports odds are designed to keep an even number of bettors on each side of the bet.

Major sports books in Las Vegas and Europe employ experienced oddsmakers to set the point spread, odds, or money line on a game. Oddsmakers must know a lot about sports and a lot about gamblers: they examine every detail of an upcoming game—including public perceptions about it—to determine which team has the better chance of winning. Several days or weeks prior to the game, the oddsmakers meet, compare information, and reach a consensus on the odds.

Here's a simple example: Team A is thought to be much better than Team B in an upcoming game. If both sides of the bet paid off the same amount of money, almost everyone would bet on Team A. The oddsmakers try to determine what odds will even out the betting. Giving Team B five-to-one odds means anyone who bets on Team B will make five times his bet if Team B wins. Team B may not have much of a chance of winning, but the increased reward makes the risk worthwhile to gamblers.

Or, depending on the sport and the country, the oddsmakers might set a money line, which is usually expressed as a "plus" or "minus" dollar amount. This is effectively the same thing as setting odds—the money line simply reflects the payoff that a bettor can expect from a winning bet.

Another way to balance the betting market is with a point spread. In this case, winning bets always pay off at one-to-one, or even odds, usually with a 10 percent vig on top, which means you would have to bet eleven dollars to win ten dollars. The point spread handicaps the game in favor of one team. In, say, football, Team A might get a spread of minus-seven. This means gamblers aren't just betting on whether Team A will win, but on whether it will do so by more than seven points.

Odds can change leading up to an event. This might indicate something significant happened, such as an injury to a key player, or it might mean that bookies are adjusting the odds because too many bets were coming in on one side. Adjusting the odds reflects their attempt to balance the betting and minimize their potential loss. Remember, a bookie isn't in this for fun and games—he's in it to make profits. And at the end of the day, he's the one who almost always wins.

WHY IS SOCCER POPULAR EVERYWHERE EXCEPT THE UNITED STATES?

Every four years, there's a sporting event that transfixes almost every country all over the entire planet. In hundreds of countries, parades are held, commerce and transportation slow to a crawl, and the home team's chances are the topic of nearly every discussion. No, it's not the Olympics—it's the World Cup. Never heard of it? Don't feel bad—neither have many of your fellow Americans. And a lot of those who have heard of it simply don't care.

Even though playing youth soccer is a veritable rite of passage in many parts of the United States, it seems that most Americans lose interest in the sport somewhere around age twelve. It's not as if adult soccer doesn't exist in this country—there's even a professional soccer league, known as Major League Soccer, which enjoys a degree of popularity and respect that's on a level with the Professional Miniature Golf Association. Yet in the rest of the world, soccer inspires passion and rabidity. The United States' indifference to soccer has baffled sports journalists and analysts for decades. Here are a few theories:

• We don't like games in which you can't use your hands. And we're a country that takes our collective hands very seriously. Some observers have pointed out that the myth of America is largely constructed upon the idea of the self-made, hardworking man—a man who uses his hands to build houses with hand-cut logs and hand-laid bricks, who uses his hands to plow the earth, plant the seeds, and bake his bread. That none of this has happened for a hundred and fifty years makes little difference to this theory's proponents.

• We don't like games without action or scoring. Soccer seems pretty boring, especially to the uninitiated. A lot of kicking the ball across a field, with very little effort being made to advance to the other team's goal. Games often end in ties or with a total tally of fewer than three goals. Yes, watching soccer for a few hours can be pretty deadening.

• We don't like prissy athletes that can't stand a little pain. Have you ever watched a soccer game? Two-thirds of it consists of players flopping lamely or gesticulating wildly when they get called for a penalty. We Americans are stand-up guys, always behaving courteously, willing to take the blame when it's our fault and the first to admit we're wrong when we're wrong. Okay, maybe not so much—as evidenced by the steroids scandal in baseball.

Or maybe the reason Americans don't like soccer is that, quite frankly, we suck at it. America has a big ego, and getting crushed in soccer by countries like Colombia and Costa Rica doesn't do much to inflate it.

The problem, though, is that if we don't pay attention to the sport, we'll probably never field a team that's good enough to be consistently competitive on the international stage. This will further suppress national interest, triggering a vicious cycle that will likely keep soccer mediocre or worse—unless an American Pelé or Diego Maradona comes along to bring it to the forefront of the country's consciousness.

In the meantime, sports analysts will continue to puzzle over why Americans don't care about soccer. It's kind of like another vexing sports question: why do so many Americans think NASCAR is worth watching?

WHICH SPORT HAS THE WORST ATHLETES?

We know what a lot of you are thinking: bowling. It's an obvious choice, but you're wrong. Yes, we know the kind of chain-smoking, beer-guzzling trainwrecks you've seen at your local bowling alley, and, yes, it's tragic. But comparing those people to pro bowlers, who need the physical and mental stamina to compete on far less forgiving lanes and bowl up to one hundred games a week, is like comparing those chunky, red-faced softball players at your local park to the major dudes in the major leagues.

And no, it's not baseball, either—John Kruk notwithstanding. (In response to a fan who chided him during his playing days for his less-than-exemplary physique, the corpulent Kruk replied, "I ain't an athlete, lady, I'm a baseball player.")

Golf is a common target for those who wish to identify nonathletes, and the sport has indeed featured some Krukian figures, such as the generously proportioned John Daly. Still, the strength and stamina it takes to get that darned ball from the tee to the hole—while walking about twenty to twenty-five miles over the course of a tournament—qualifies as athletic prowess. (You snicker, but when was the last time you walked twenty-five miles in a week?)

How about the luge? Now we're getting somewhere. Who among us hasn't spent an entire Sunday afternoon "practicing the luge" (i.e., prostrate on the couch in front of the TV, watching other people sweat)? Turns out, though, that real lugers have tremendous upper-body strength and spend their off-seasons lifting weights and swimming. Who knew?

So we turn to curling, which, as we are all aware, is basically just shuffleboard for aging Canadians who haven't yet broken their hips. At the 2006 Winter Olympics, United States curler Scott Baird competed at the age of fifty-four. And yet, there is agility involved—it's kind of like bowling on ice. And did you see that "women of curling" nude calendar that made a splash during those same 2006 Olympics? We defy you to tell us that those bodies weren't athletic.

Okay, time to get serious. Which sport has the worst athletes? We planned to choose darts, which requires participants to spend as much time as possible in bars, where breaking a sweat has more to do with the TV lighting than the action. But then we stumbled upon the Cyberathlete Professional League (CPL). That's right: professional video gamers posing as athletes.

Sure, this seems like a typical case of the jocks picking on the nerds. But the CPL (before it folded in 2008) went to great lengths to portray itself as a real, big-time sports league, right down to its red, white, and blue logo that mimicked the classic NBA and Major League Baseball logos—a silhouetted figure (seated, of course) wearing headphones and pumping one fist in the air exultantly while the other hand daintily fingers a mouse. In other words, they were asking for it. A sport of computer geeks. A sport with an "official pizza" (Pizza Hut). That's the sport with the worst athletes.

WHY DO GROWN MEN WANT TO PLAY WITH TOYS?

Every Christmas, in households across America, little kids wake up at the crack of dawn. Silently, they creep downstairs to see what Santa has left them. They hear noises in the living room— clicks and rasps, a murmur. Is it possible that Santa is still there? They reach the doorway, peek in, and find . . . Dad, playing with the video game system that was supposed to be for the kids. Come on, Dad!

Of course, it's commonly held wisdom that most men are just big kids at heart. And like kids, they need their toys, whether their playthings are video games, smart phones, or sports cars. But why is this? After all, everybody knows that the adult world is a sober, stressful place with no room for childish games.

Maybe not. Play theorists suggest that toys and games aid mental development in children and adults alike. For children, games act as staging grounds for the adult world. (They require cognitive skills like understanding rules or strategy, and social skills like cooperation and communication.) But this development doesn't stop at adulthood. According to scientists, playing with toys can help "potentiate novelty." (This is a fancy way of saying that it can inspire creativity, generate new ideas, and help adults approach problems in new ways.) In fact, Albert Einstein himself stated that play is essential to any productive thought. And who's going to argue with him?

But why do men seem more apt to play with toys than women? While the reasons haven't been extensively studied, one explanation may lie in the respective roles that men and women have traditionally played in society. For most of modern history, men have been the wage-earners, the handlers of weighty responsibilities—the very ones for whom "potentiating novelty" is the most important. And as bacon-bringers and novelty-potentiators, they deserve nothing less than a hot meal when they get home from the office, a nice martini, and, obviously, a sixteen-thousand-dollar stereo system. A woman, on the other hand, was trained by society to play the role of caregiver, of homemaker, of nurturer. There was no time—or excuse—for frivolity when the laundry needed washing, the kids needed bathing, and the husband's martini needed mixing.

Of course, most people would call this assumption a load of rubbish. Regardless, as gender roles continue to evolve, there may be a correlating shift in how men and women approach leisure. And this may be a good thing for everybody because in addition to their sociological importance, toys may also have health benefits.

Being an adult can be stressful—and stress, doctors tell us, is one of the worst things for our bodies. Enter toys. Play therapists suggest that one of the best ways of reducing stress is to hit the arcade or pick up a hobby. In fact, an intense game of air-hockey at that arcade may have health benefits beyond mere stress reduction. Indeed, mounting evidence suggests that active use of the brain—through the creative thinking or puzzle-solving involved with many computer games, for example—may help stave off degenerative brain diseases like Alzheimer's. This is good news for the 53 percent of adults who reported to the Pew Center in 2008 that they routinely play video games. So go ahead, Dad—it's okay to play a little Xbox on Christmas morning. Just give the kids a turn once in a while.

WHAT DOES DONKEY KONG HAVE TO DO WITH DONKEYS?

Before entering the strange new world of video games in the late 1970s, Nintendo was a small but established Japanese toy company that specialized in producing playing cards. Early in its video game venture, the company found itself stuck with about two thousand arcade cabinets for an unpopular game called *Radar Scope*. Nintendo's president tapped a young staff artist named Shigeru Miyamoto to create a new game that enabled the company to reuse the cabinets.

Miyamato developed an action game in which the player was a little jumping construction worker (named Jumpman, naturally) who had to rescue his lady friend from a barrel-chucking ape. Thanks to the classic movie monster, nothing says "rampaging gorilla" like "Kong," in either English or Japanese, so that part of the name was a no-brainer.

Miyamoto also wanted to include a word that suggested "stubborn" in the title, so he turned to his handy Japanese-to-English dictionary, which listed "donkey" as a synonym. (Several English speakers at Nintendo did point out that "Donkey Kong" didn't mean what Miyamoto thought it did, but the name stuck anyway.)

Silly as the name was, things worked out exceedingly well for everyone involved. *Donkey Kong* hit arcades in 1981 and became one of the most successful games in the world, defining Nintendo as a premier video game company in the process. Jumpman changed his name to Mario, became a plumber, and grew into the most famous video game character ever. Miyamoto established himself as the Steven Spielberg of game designers, racking up hit after hit.

Sadly, there has yet to be a hit game starring a donkey. Maybe someday Miyamoto will get around to designing one.

WHICH SPORT HAS THE GREATEST ATHLETES?

Sometimes the simplest questions are the most complicated to answer. Even if you agree on the criteria for which sport has the greatest athletes—strength, agility, endurance, coordination, all of the above, or some of the above—you come up with no consensus on the answer. So let's start by running down some of the experts' opinions.

Canada's Sun Media newspapers published a series of articles in 2007 in which five sports were analyzed—basketball, baseball, football, hockey, and soccer—and the arguments for soccer players being the greatest athletes seemed the most persuasive. Soccer players run six miles or more per game, combining jogging and sprinting for ninety minutes. There are changes of direction, vertical jumps, astounding acts of agility, one-on-one battles that often get physical, and the need to be just as sharp in the ninetieth minute as in the first. The writer called soccer the most physically demanding team sport.

However, Sun Media's own medical expert, Dr. Bob Litchfield, medical director of the Fowler Kennedy Sports Medicine Clinic at the University of Western Ontario, cast his vote for basketball because of the wear and tear players in that sport—particularly NBA guards—must endure.

When the scope is widened beyond major sports, other athletes make powerful cases. The *St. Petersburg Times* in Florida did research in 2004 and decided the toughest sport is—drum roll, please—water polo. Sorry, but there's something anticlimactic about that one. For another perspective, the *Times* talked to Dr. Peter Davis, director of coaching and sports sciences for the United States Olympic Committee (USOC). Davis presumably has the kind of broad-based practical experience necessary to render an objective answer. "My vote for world's best athlete? I'd say an Australian Rules football player," Davis said. "Then again, I'm biased. I'm from Australia." Davis also noted that USOC scientists consider synchronized swimming the most grueling sport. "Try treading water for a minute while making perfectly choreographed movements. And, oh yeah, do it upside down, under water," he said.

Men's Journal magazine did its top ten in 2003 and decided on gymnastics, followed by the Ironman triathlon, rock climbing, hockey, bull riding, boxing, rugby, decathlon, water polo, and football. No soccer, basketball, Australian Rules football, endurance bicycling, or synchronized swimming. See how hard it is to find a consensus? Then there are the oh-so-clever pundits who claim that racehorses are the best athletes. Yes, they're powerful, graceful, and fast. But have you ever seen a horse hit a curveball?

As you can see, the answer to this question is completely subjective. Our vote goes for basketball, which combines all of soccer's strength and agility needs with most of its endurance demands, then layers on the whole upper-body thing plus equal or greater degrees of physical contact. Then again, we could just throw up our hands and vote for poker players. After all, they have to worry about hemorrhoids. And those things are painful.

WHY DO GOLFERS WEAR SUCH SILLY CLOTHES?

In most of the major sports, athletes don't have much choice when it comes to what they wear. Basketball, football, baseball, and hockey teams all have uniforms. But other athletes aren't so lucky (and neither are their fans). Golfers, for example, are allowed to choose their own garb, leading to a parade of "uniforms" that look as if they were stitched together by a band of deranged clowns.

Why big-time golfers wear such hideous clothes is a source of bewilderment. Some apologists blame it on the Scots. Golf, after all, was supposedly invented by shepherds in Scotland back in the twelfth century, and it almost goes without saying that a sport born in a country where man-skirts are considered fashionable is doomed from the start. We'd like to point out that we are no longer in twelfth-century Scotland—so let's move on, people.

But history may indeed play a role in golf's repeated fashion disasters. Kings and queens were reputed to have hit the links in the sixteenth and seventeenth centuries, and by the late nineteenth century, golf was a popular pastime amongst the nobility of England and Scotland. The nobility, however, wasn't exactly known for its athletic prowess. The other "sports" many of these noblemen participated in were activities like steeplechase (which has its own awful fashion), and so most early golfers had no idea what types of clothes would be appropriate for an athletic endeavor. Early golfers simply took to the links wearing the fashionable attire of the day—attire that, unfortunately, included breeches and ruffled cravats (these were like neckties).

The tradition of wearing stuffy, silly attire continued into the twentieth century (as did the tradition of wealthy, paunchy white guys playing the sport), with awful sweaters and clashing polyester pants replacing the ruffled cravats and knee-length knickers. Yet, remarkably, modern golfers take umbrage at the stereotype that duffers have no sense of fashion. According to one golf wag, the knock on golfers for being the world's worst-dressed athletes is unfair because nowadays almost everybody wears Dockers and polo shirts. (We'll pause while that gem sinks in.)

To be fair, the dreadful golf fashions of the 1970s and 1980s have given way to a more benign blandness that is at least less offensive, if not remotely what anybody would call "stylish." Of course, all fashion is less offensive than it was in the 1970s and 1980s, so perhaps golf fashion is proportionally no better.

"Golf," Mark Twain once complained, "is a good walk spoiled." We love Mark Twain, but we have to say that spoiling a good walk is the least of golf's transgressions.

HOW COME A HOCKEY PUCK IS SO HARD TO FOLLOW?

If you have trouble following a hockey puck as it darts all over the ice, you're probably relatively new to the sport. Spectators who are indoctrinated enough to have lost a tooth or two in the stands—or at their local watering holes—during heated arguments about their favorite hockey teams have little trouble tracking that black blur, mostly because they can anticipate the action.

Hockey bills itself as the fastest sport around, and not just because of the puck. True, in the National Hockey League (NHL), a great scorer's slap shot can easily top one hundred miles per hour—in the 1960s, Chicago Blackhawks star Bobby Hull had a slapshot clocked at 120 miles per hour and a wrist shot at 105 miles per hour.

The players themselves are a blur, too. They skate at thirty miles per hour in sprinting situations and at twenty miles per hour when they're cruising down the ice. Such speed is rarely seen in the "foot" team sports, such as football, basketball, and baseball. So the frenetic action around the puck is part of what makes that black disc so hard to follow.

Still, the puck isn't completely innocent in this. At one inch thick and three inches in diameter, it's much smaller than a football or basketball. Hockey fans learn to keep tabs on the puck as they pick up on the nuances of the sport. They anticipate charges down the ice and take notice of how players position themselves for scoring opportunities, and they grow to appreciate the "nonpuck" plays, like checking and boxing out.

Watching hockey on television can be a challenge, and the Fox network tried to help with its use of the "smart puck" in the mid-1990s. Fox used the wonders of modern technology to transform the puck into a colored dot that had an easy-to-follow trail. The smart puck was widely panned for its distracting effect on the games. In fact, the only thing smart about it was that it went into cold storage after Fox's TV contract with the NHL expired. But the smart puck did have some value: it taught us that sometimes harder is better.

IN SOCCER, WHY ARE YELLOW CARDS YELLOW AND RED CARDS RED?

And Why Aren't There Any Green Cards?

Considering that the game of soccer has existed in its modern form since the mid-nineteenth century, it's rather strange that no formal penalty system—i.e., red cards and yellow cards—was put into place until the latter part of the twentieth century. The situation is stranger still when you consider the innocuous way in which red cards and yellow cards came to be.

Ken Aston, a headmaster at a British school, was sitting at a stoplight after attending a World Cup quarterfinal between England and Argentina in 1966 when an idea that would change soccer popped into his head. "As I drove down Kensington High Street, the traffic light turned red," Aston said. "I thought, 'Yellow, take it easy; red, stop, you're off.' "

Aston's brainstorm was prompted by the lack of formal, announced penalties in soccer at the time. As ridiculous as it seems, players could be penalized in a soccer match or ejected without any sort of declaration from the referee.

In the England versus Argentina match, numerous players had been ejected by the referee without being told of their infraction. Aston knew the obvious: soccer needed a formalized way to keep players and fans informed of infractions.

The global soccer community embraced Aston's idea. The system of yellow and red cards was adopted and implemented in time for the 1970 World Cup in Mexico City. For those who don't follow soccer closely, here is a quick tutorial on why a ref would pull out a yellow card or red card.

A yellow card is presented to a player as a warning after any of the following infractions:

• Unsportsmanlike conduct
• Dissent by word or actions
• Persistent rule-breaking
• Delaying the restart of play
• Defending a corner kick or free kick too closely
• Entering or leaving the field without referee permission

A red card is given if a player receives two yellow cards in a match, or when any of the following occurs:

• Serious foul play
• Violence
• Spitting
• Denying an obvious goal-scoring opportunity by deliberately handling the ball
• Fouling an opponent to prevent an obvious goal-scoring opportunity
• Offensive or threatening language

If shown a red card, a player is "sent off" and cannot be replaced, forcing his or her team to compete with one player less than the other team. Players shown the red card are not allowed to remain on the sideline or bench—they have to go straight to the locker room.

Since Aston's epiphany, the practice of issuing colored cards has been adopted by other sports besides soccer, including volleyball, rugby, field hockey, lacrosse, and handball. In rugby, a yellow card gets you sent to the "sin bin," which is like the penalty box in hockey.

In soccer, a yellow card will get you a break from the game. It sounds genteel enough, just as Aston imagined it should be while idling at that traffic light. The reality, however, has been something different, especially in soccer-crazed Europe. Sometimes an ill-issued yellow card can spark a near-riot, which begs the question: why doesn't soccer have a "sin bin," too . . . for its hooligan fans?

WHY IS A ROUND OF GOLF EIGHTEEN HOLES?

Is It Because There Are Eighteen Shots in a Bottle of Whiskey?

Although that theory has a kind of sense, it's not true. A fifth of Scotch is about twenty-six ounces, and if you break that into eighteen shots, you'll have some seriously large snorts of booze. No, the answer is as simple as this: there are eighteen holes in an official round of golf because the Royal and Ancient Golf Club of St. Andrews in Scotland told its members so in 1858.

This is just one of the ways that the spiritual home of golf has influenced the game we play today. Now, we're not saying the R&A stated that every official round of golf had to be eighteen holes—it only stipulated that this was the case on its course. But since we're talking St. Andrews, one of the courses on which the British Open is played, and because the R&A has been so influential in other respects, the formality caught on.

There's actually nothing intrinsically right about eighteen holes—it's just what St. Andrews' members tended to play. For much of the club's history, the course didn't even have eighteen distinct holes. Until 1764, St. Andrews had twelve holes, most of which ran along the water, "links" style. Members played them in order, then played ten of them backward, for a round of twenty-two.

That year, members decided to shorten a round to eighteen holes. It took nearly a hundred years for the club to standardize this as an official round, though its members continued to play rounds of various lengths for their own fun. In 1867, nine years after St. Andrews made eighteen official, Carnoustie Golf Links (another legendary course in Scotland) added eight holes to make eighteen. The trend had begun.

Before all this, courses came in every configuration imaginable, usually featuring between a few and a dozen holes. Golf had not yet become the ritualized game that it is today, so players didn't feel compelled to play a specific number of holes. Curiously, there is a trend developing today toward returning to less-formalized play. A round of eighteen holes was fine for well-heeled members of the R&A, as well as for American dads in the 1950s through the 1980s, who felt entitled to a full Saturday at the golf course after a hard week at the office. But today's dads are schlepping the kids to soccer on Saturdays while overworked moms get a break, and golf courses have had to improvise. Some now offer "6 after 6"—six holes of golf and a burger after 6:00 p.m.—just to get folks out to play. It's possible that someday eighteen holes will seem as antiquated as St. Andrews' original twelve do to us now.

WHAT IS THE DIFFERENCE BETWEEN BILLIARDS AND POOL?

It's a trick question: there is no difference. Billiards is a catchall term that includes a number of games that are played on a rectangular, felt-topped table and involve hitting balls with a long stick (the cue). Some of the more popular games in this category include French (or carom) billiards, English billiards, snooker, and pocket billiards (which is the game you know as pool).

If you're a pool player accustomed to the satisfying clunk of a ball dropping into one of the pockets, French billiards will probably make you feel like you're in that weird, abstract foreign film that you were forced to watch on a bad date. There are no pockets, and there are only three balls: one white; one red; and one either yellow or white, with a little red dot on it. Either of the white balls (or the yellow ball) can serve as the cue ball. The point of the game (if there really is a point) is for the cue ball to hit the other two balls in succession. This is a carom. Each time a carom is accomplished, a point is awarded. The player who manages to keep from dying of boredom the longest is the winner.

English billiards incorporates the same three balls as French billiards, but the table features the six pockets familiar to pool players—one in each corner, and one on each of the long sides of the rectangle. There are four ways to score: you can hit the two balls in succession, a la French billiards; you can hit the red ball into a pocket; you can hit the other cue ball into a pocket; or you can hit the cue ball against another ball before the cue ball goes into a pocket. The winner is the player who can tally the score without using a slide rule.

Snooker also is played on a table with six pockets, but there are twenty-two balls: fifteen red balls, six balls of various colors that are assigned numbers, and a cue ball. After you knock a red ball into a pocket, you're allowed to pocket one of the numbered balls. The ball's number is added to your score, and then the ball is returned to the table. Then you have to pocket another red ball before going after a numbered ball, and so on. The winner is the player who can go the longest without giggling at any mention of the word "snooker."

Pocket billiards, or pool, involves fifteen numbered balls and a cue ball. Pool is played in bars, bowling alleys, and basement rec rooms across North America by people in various states of inebriation. Popular variations of pool include the games rotation, straight pool, and eight ball. Scoring systems differ, but the point of each game ultimately is to avoid finger injuries between games, when angry, drunken losing players engage in the time-honored tradition of venting their frustrations by hitting the remaining balls way harder than anyone would ever need to hit them.

WHY ARE THREE STRAIGHT BOWLING STRIKES CALLED A TURKEY?

We love bowling. Love the mustaches, the tinted glasses, the fingerless gloves. We love that air-vent thingy on the ball rack, and we love the swirling balls that are inscribed with names like Lefty and Dale. We love the satin shirts and multi-colored shoes (okay, maybe not the shoes so much). But what we love most are the terms. The Dutch 200, the Brooklyn strike, the Cincinnati, the Jersey, and the Greek Church. We have no idea what any of these terms mean, but we love them all the same.

Believe it or not, bowling wasn't always the sexy, hip sport played by highly trained athletes that it is today. Some historians trace bowling's roots back to 3200 BC, while others place its origin in Europe in the third century AD. Regardless, some form of bowling has been popular for centuries. For much of this history, however, bowling didn't have a particularly sterling reputation. Quite the opposite: legend holds that King Edward III banned bowling after his good-for-nothing soldiers kept skipping archery practice to roll. And well into the nineteenth century, American towns were passing laws that forbid bowling, largely because of the gambling that went along with it.

Despite these attempts at suppression—or perhaps because of them—bowling increased in popularity. In 1895, the American Bowling Congress (now known as the United States Bowling Congress) was formed, and local and regional bowling clubs began proliferating. It was around this time that the term "Turkey" came into being.

In an attempt to cash in on the burgeoning popularity of the newly sanctioned sport, as well as draw customers, many bowling alley proprietors began offering a free live turkey to bowlers who successfully rolled three strikes in a row during Thanksgiving or Christmas week. Sadly, live turkeys are no longer awarded at bowling alleys, although the tradition of shouting "Turkey" when somebody manages three strikes in a row continues.

So the next time you cry "fowl" at your local bowling alley, you can take pride in knowing that you're continuing a time-honored tradition. Now if we could just figure out who decided two-toned bowling shoes were a good idea, we'd really be on to something.

WHAT HAPPENED WHEN A DUEL ENDED IN A TIE?

Ah, the romantic days of yore, when courtly ladies rode in well-appointed horse-drawn carriages and gentlemen who knew the meaning of honor slapped each other with white calfskin gloves and then met at dawn to fire nicely-polished guns at one another. To quote poet/rocker Ray Davies, "Where have all the good times gone?"

Back in the good old days, if a gentleman felt insulted, he didn't stoop to starting a shouting match, a fistfight, or even a flame war online. Instead, he had recourse to a duel. Dueling, which originated in sixteenth-century Italy before gaining popularity throughout Europe, generally followed a protocol. The insulted party would throw down his glove before demanding "satisfaction" from the other party. Apparently, this satisfaction could only be obtained by shooting at him.

What happened if a duel ended in a tie? Who won satisfaction?

Actually, duels that ended in ties were rather commonplace. Not all duels were fought "to the death." Some could be fought "to the blood," in which the first man who drew blood from his opponent was the victor. In the case of pistol dueling, "to the blood" meant that each man was allowed only one shot. (Often, the act of the duel itself was enough to save the honor of the participants, and many a duel ended with the two parties simply firing into the air.)

Pistol dueling is what most people think of when they imagine duels, though before the advent of guns, weapons such as swords were used. And even after pistols became fashionable, gentlemen sometimes chose other weapons to defend their honor. One apocryphal tale tells of an aborted duel in the mid-nineteenth century between Otto von Bismarck and his nemesis Rudolf Virchow, in which sausages (oh, those wacky Germans!) were chosen as the weapon.

One of the most famous duels that ended in a tie occurred in 1826 and was between two United States senators, Henry Clay of Mississippi and John Randolph of Virginia. Clay was known as a firebrand, and when he and Randolph disagreed on an issue, Clay demanded satisfaction. The much-ballyhooed duel took place on April 8. Each senator was allowed one shot; naturally, they both missed. It's yet another example of the inability of politicians to do much of anything right.

Duels are no longer an accepted social custom; virtually every country has outlawed them. Still, there's no law against throwing down one's glove and demanding satisfaction.

HOW DID COLLEGE AND PRO FOOTBALL BECOME THE MONSTERS THEY ARE TODAY?

The game of football today bears little resemblance to the disorganized brawls of the late 1800s. As many college rivalries pass their hundredth meetings, football has trumped baseball as America's favorite sport.

1861: The first documented football game (essentially rugby) is played at the University of Toronto.

1869: An era begins as Princeton travels to Rutgers for a rousing game of "soccer football." The field is 120 yards long by 75 yards wide, about 25 percent longer and wider than the modern field. It plays more like soccer than modern football, and with 25 players on a side, the field is a crowded place. Rutgers prevails 6–4.

1874: McGill University (of Montreal) and Harvard play a hybrid version of rugby. The rule changes soon affect the game in the United States.

1875: The game ball officially becomes an egg-shape rugby ball. Henceforth the field is supposed to be 100 yards long by 53.5 yards wide (though this won't be fully standard for some years), so teams are cut to 15 players per side. Referees are added to the game.

1876: With the addition of the crossbar, goal posts now look like an H.

1880–1885: The modern game's fundamentals are introduced. A downs system goes into use (five yards in three downs equals a first down), along with the scrimmage line and yard lines. Teams are now 11 on a side. Major changes to scoring: a field goal is worth five points, a touchdown and conversion count four points each, and a safety is two points. The first play-calling signals and planned plays come about.

1892: Desperate to beat the Pittsburgh Athletic Club team, Allegheny Athletic Association leaders create the professional football player by hiring William Walter "Pudge" Heffelfinger to play for their team. That's right: Pudge Heffelfinger. Heffelfinger plays a pivotal role in AAA's 4–0 victory.

1894: The officiating crew is increased to three: a referee and two bodyguards, also known as the umpire and linesman.

1896: Only one backfield man may now be in motion before the snap, and he can't be moving forward.

1897: A touchdown now counts as five points.

1902: College football is getting a little unbalanced as Michigan, having outscored its regular schedule 501–0, drubs Stanford 49–0 in the first Rose Bowl. The first African American professional football player takes the field: Charles Follis of the Shelby (Ohio) Athletic Club.

1905: Disgusted at the mortality rate among college football players, Teddy Roosevelt tells the Ivy League schools: "Fix this blood sport, or I'll ban it." Rules Committee (forerunner of the NCAA) comes into being and legalizes the forward pass, bans mass plays responsible for brutish pileups and deaths, establishes the neutral zone along the line of scrimmage, and prohibits players from locking arms.

1909: Now a field goal is worth three points. This rule will stand, but the distances, hash marks, and goal posts will change many more times. In Canada, the first Grey Cup game is played—at this phase, it's a collegiate event.

1910: Seven players must now be on the line of scrimmage when the ball is snapped, establishing the basic offensive formation concept. The forward pass becomes commonplace in college football.

1912: Rules Committee determines that a touchdown is worth six points, and it adds a fourth down. It is now practical to punt.

1921: Fans hear the first commercially sponsored radio broadcast of a game, with University of Pittsburgh beating West Virginia 21–13.

1922: The American Professional Football Association becomes the National Football League (NFL).

1932: The NFL begins keeping statistics. Collegiate football doesn't see the benefits of official stat keeping until 1937.

1933: There is a major NFL rule change: the passer can throw from anywhere behind scrimmage. (Before this, he had to be five yards behind scrimmage.)

1934: The modern football takes its current shape after a couple of decades of gradual evolution from the egg-like rugby ball.

1937: College football players must now have numbers on the fronts and backs of their jerseys.

1939: The Brooklyn Dodgers–Philadelphia Eagles game is the first to be beamed into the few New York homes that can afford TV sets in this Depression year. Helmets become mandatory in college football, and the pros follow within a decade.

1941: It's the end of the drop-kick score. Ray McLean boots a conversion off the turf in the NFL championship game. (Actually, it wasn't the last one kicked. In 2005, Doug Flutie created a sensation by doing it again.)

1946: The NFL's first major rival league, the All-America Football Conference (AAFC), begins play. It lasts four seasons, with the Cleveland Browns winning all four titles.

1950: Rules now permit unlimited free substitution, ushering in platoon football (exclusive offensive or defensive squads).

1951: First coast-to-coast TV broadcast of an NFL game as the Los Angeles Rams face the Cleveland Browns in the league championship game. Face masks show up in the college game.

1956: The NFL penalizes face masking (except for the ball carrier, who can be slammed to the turf by the face until 1960).

1958: In college football, a run or pass for conversion now counts two points.

1960: The American Football League (AFL), the NFL's new rival, begins play. Everyone derides it as inferior, just like the old AAFC.

1967: The NFL offsets goal posts with a recessed curved pole in a "slingshot" shape. Super Bowl I is played: the Green Bay Packers beat the Kansas City Chiefs, 35–10.

1970: The AFL wins the Super Bowl, then merges into the NFL, creating the biggest sports-marketing titan of all time. (Ten modern NFL teams trace heritage to the AFL.)

1974: The NFL adds sudden-death overtime for regular-season games, moves the goal posts to the back of the end zone, moves kickoffs back from the 40- to the 35-yard line, and spots the ball at the line of scrimmage for missed field goals beyond the 20. Pass defense rules now restrict defenders, opening up the air game.

1975: Kicker/quarterback George Blanda of the Oakland Raiders finally hangs up his cleats at the age of 48.

1979–1980: No more blocking below the waist on kicks, refs are to whistle a play dead when a player has the quarterback in a death grip but has not yet slammed him to the turf, and personal-foul rules tighten up.

1987: Arena Football League season starts with four teams: the Chicago Bruisers, Denver Dynamite, Pittsburgh Gladiators, and Washington Commandos.

1988: The NFL increases the play clock to 45 seconds between plays. Eventually this is shortened to 40 seconds. College still uses the 25-second play clock.

1991: The World League of American Football (WLAF)—history's first non–North American league—begins in Europe as a sort of NFL minor league. Europeans prefer soccer.

1994: Professional football institutes the option of either running or passing for two points (instead of kicking for one) after a touchdown.

1999: The NFL begins using an instant replay challenge system, thus eliminating officiating errors forever. (We're employing irony here.)

2007: The NFL Europa, successor to the WLAF, finally shuts down, as Europeans still prefer soccer.

1. Where did the territorial-capture board game Go originate, 4,000 years ago?
a. India
b. China
c. Japan
d. Persia

2. During a serve in American racquetball, what is the first surface the ball must hit after the racket?
a. The ceiling
b. One of the side walls
c. The front wall
d. The front floor

3. How many unique numbers are used in Sudoku?
a. 81
b. 6
c. 9
d. 27

4. When did Ralph Samuelson invent water skiing?
a. 1942
b. 1842
c. 1922
d. 1932

5. What is the minimum number of moves needed to achieve checkmate in chess?
a. 2
b. 7
c. 12
d. 13

6. Which sport is not represented in the Olympics?
a. Basketball
b. Cricket
c. Dressage
d. Handball

7. Sam Groth hit the fastest tennis serve ever recorded in 2012. How fast was it?
a. 98 miles per hour
b. 133 miles per hour
c. 163 miles per hour
d. 263 miles per hour

8. Who holds the record for most points (100) in a single NBA game?
a. Wilt Chamberlain
b. Elgin Baylor
c. Kobe Bryant
d. Michael Jordan

9. Who invented the game of Scrabble™?
a. Alan Max Wordman
b. Al "Pal" Gustav Flugel
c. Alfred Neumann
d. Alfred Mosher Butts

10. When Bingo started some time around 1929, what was it called?
a. Beano
b. Bing Bing
c. Bongo
d. Bang Whoa

1.
b. China

2.
c. The front wall

3.
c. 9

4.
c. 1922

5.
a. 2

6.
b. Cricket

7.
c. 163 miles per hour

8.
a. Wilt Chamberlain

9.
d. Alfred Mosher Butts

10.
a. Beano

TIMELY MATTERS

THIRTY DAYS HATH SEPTEMBER, SOMETHING SOMETHING SOMETHING

Humans are the only creatures with an abstract sense of time. Okay, dogs understand "now" and cats have a great grasp of "never," but we're the only ones that get "when." Even so, there's something peculiar about the way we think about time, divide it up, and describe it to each other. And the more you examine clocks, calendars, and units of time, the more you realize that where time is concerned, nothing is absolutely certain. Why do we have things like time zones and Daylight Saving Time, anyway? You'll know in a New York minute.

DOES A SUNDIAL WORK WHEN IT'S CLOUDY OUTSIDE?

Life in ancient Sumer (home of the Sumerians) was sweet indeed. Missed a deadline? Late for school? Strolled into work an hour late? So what? For half the year, nobody had a clue what time it was. That's because a sundial—the primary timekeeping device of ancient times—doesn't work without the sun.

Sundials are one of oldest timekeeping tools in human history; primitive versions have been discovered that date back to 3500 BC. In Egypt, enormous granite sundials, known as Cleopatra's Needles—were used to keep time; later, the mathematically inclined Greeks devised elaborate sundials—such as the famous Tower of the Winds in Athens—which (like the Egyptian sundials before them) divided the day into twelve hours.

Of course, a sundial can only do so much. As most of us recall from grade-school science projects, a sundial is a relatively simple instrument—essentially, it's a stick in the ground. Making matters worse, thanks to the changing angle of the earth throughout the year, the lengths and positions of the shadows cast by a sundial are inconsistent from season to season, even week to week. A further drawback—and the one we're addressing here—is that the sundial requires a shadow in order to tell the time, which renders it utterly useless on cloudy days. No sun means no shadows, which equaled havoc for the schedule makers of yore.

With all their limitations, sundials were destined to go the way of the dodo. (Or perhaps dodos went the way of the sundial.)

By the fourteenth century, the mechanical clock was invented. Sundials were reduced to excruciating science-class projects and kitschy garden ornaments, and the chronically late were deprived of one of history's all-time great excuses.

HOW COME THE ANCIENT ROMANS BEGAN THEIR YEAR IN MARCH?

The Romans claimed that Rome's first king, Romulus, came up with the first calendar and that he decided the year would begin on the spring equinox. Most years, this falls on the day we call March 20. Since Rome was supposedly founded in 735 BC, that became year one of the Roman calendar.

We can only guess why the spring equinox was chosen. Maybe it had meaning because the world comes to life again after a cold winter: flowers bloom, greenery appears, and birds build nests. But there's a problem with that theory: no other European cultures began their year with spring. Some of the ancient Greeks began their year with the summer solstice (June 21); the Celts picked November 1 as New Year's Day; and the Germanic tribes started their year in the dead of winter, much as we do today. Bottom line: we don't know why the Roman year started in springtime.

The original name of March was *Martius*, which was an homage to the god of war, Mars. Romulus designated only ten months for the year, though. Why? Romulus liked the number ten. He organized his administration, his senate, his land, and his military legions into units of ten, so why not his calendar, too?

However, ten times thirty or thirty-one (the designated numbers of days of the months back then) made for a pretty short year. Records don't survive to tell us how the people of Rome managed, but within a couple of generations, two more months were added to the calendar.

Did the year continue to start on the spring equinox? Not exactly. Maintaining the calendar was the duty of priestly officials, who could add days when needed. Over the centuries, corrupt priests and politicians manipulated the Roman calendar to extend political terms of office and delay important votes in the assembly—they didn't really give a hoot if it ended up astronomically accurate. The first month of every year was March, but it didn't always correlate to the March that we know—it was sometimes as many as three months off.

Julius Caesar—who was once one of those priestly officials— revised the calendar after he took control of Rome. He brought it more in line with the calendar that we know today; in fact, he even added a leap year. But Caesar's leap year was a little different from ours: once every four years, February 24 was counted twice. Those wacky Romans.

WAS A DAY ALWAYS 24 HOURS LONG?

From almost the first moment humans decided that a day needed more segmentation than the obvious day and night, twenty-four has been the number of choice. The practice began thirty-five hundred years ago, with the invention of the Egyptian sundial. Before then, humans had little interest in specifying the time of day. It was enough to differentiate between morning and evening by using an obelisk—a four-sided monument that cast a westward shadow in the pre-noon hours and an eastward shadow as evening approached.

The sundial divided a day into twelve hours of light and twelve hours of darkness—though, of course, it was capable of displaying the time only during sunlight hours. The Egyptians marked an hour of twilight at sunrise, an hour of twilight at sunset, and ten hours in between. Nighttime hours were approximated by the use of decan stars (stars that rise in the hours before dawn). Twelve decan stars rise in the Egyptian sky during the summer months. Historians believe that these stars might be the reason the earliest timekeepers chose to base their sundials on the number twelve.

The hour itself did not have a specific, set length until the second century BC—thirteen hundred years later. Until then, the length of the hour changed as the seasons changed. During winter months, nighttime hours were longer; during summer months, daytime hours were longer. In the second century BC, the Greek astronomer Hipparchus divided the day into twenty-four equal segments.

Keeping time was still an inexact science for the common man. Until the invention of the modern clock, just about everyone simply divided a day into twelve hours of daylight and twelve of darkness. The modern mechanical clock, which keeps time by the regulated swinging of a pendulum, was conceptualized by Galileo, the sixteenth- and seventeenth-century mathematician and philosopher. The first such timepiece was built by Dutch scientist Christiaan Huygens in the seventeenth century.

In the centuries since, clocks have become increasingly precise, culminating with invention of the atomic clock in the twentieth century. Finally, the entire population of the world is in sync. Hipparchus would be proud.

WHY DO THEY CALL IT THE DARK AGES?

Okay, so maybe the Roman Empire crumbled and all of its advances in urban refinement—in fundamental areas such as agriculture, roads, and sanitation—fell into steep decline.

So maybe a few Germanic tribes accosted southern and western Europe and wreaked a little havoc on the culture and the social order. So maybe there was a plague. The truth is, anyone can have a bad half-millennium. Do we have to rub salt into the wounds and call the whole messy affair the Dark Ages? Is that really fair?

Actually, modern-day historians generally don't use that term anymore. The period that ran from roughly AD 500 to 1000 is now referred to in less pejorative terms, such as "Late Antiquity" or the "Early Middle Ages." For a while, the term "Dark Ages" was co-opted from its original, negative meaning and was used to refer to the fact that historical detail of the era was a bit sketchy—but that never really caught on.

The notion of a specific period of time that we now know as the Middle Ages originated with Renaissance historians. As the Renaissance got into full swing in the fourteenth century, Italian humanist historians sought to link their movement with the classical philosophical movements of Rome and Greece (beginning around the fifth century BC). They needed a name for the downtime between the two movements, so they called it "the Dark Ages," thumbed their noses at it, and then went about the task of showing how enlightened they were.

Fourteenth-century Italian poet-scholar Petrarch is said to have coined the term "Dark Ages." It doesn't appear that he actually used that exact phrase himself, but he is still credited with introducing the idea of a time when knowledge of the great works of classical antiquity faded into obscurity, with nothing new being offered in its place—even if modern historians strenuously disagree with his dismal assessment.

WHY DO THE CHINESE REPRESENT EACH YEAR WITH AN ANIMAL?

To Westerners, 2015 was the twelve months between December 2014 and January 2016. But to the Chinese, it was the Year of the Sheep. Chinese New Year traditionally falls in late January or early February and kicks off a period that's named for a particular animal. If you're not familiar with the Chinese zodiac—or haven't been to a Chinese restaurant where it's colorfully displayed on placemats—you may be wondering how this curious tradition got started.

The Chinese zodiac is based on the lunisolar calendar, which is governed by the solar year and the phases of the moon. It assigns an animal to hours within a day, periods within a year, and individual years. The Chinese zodiac rotates on a twelve-year cycle and the animals, in order, are: rat, ox, tiger, rabbit or hare, dragon, snake, horse, sheep or ram, monkey, rooster, dog, and pig. Each animal has specific traits that are said to determine a person's personality as well as foretell events.

And while the Chinese zodiac's exact origin is unknown, there are many theories about why these particular animals were chosen. One holds that they're related to an ancient system of telling time known as the Ten Celestial Stems and the Twelve Earthly Branches. It was used in China as early as the Shang Dynasty, possibly around 1122 BC. Familiar animals were chosen to represent each of the Twelve Earthly Branches because the average person of the day could not read or perform the calculations that were necessary to determine the time.

In this system, the animals are ordered based on their number of hooves or toes, and they alternate between odd and even numbers. For example, a rat has five toes on its back feet, so it is the first animal. The second animal, the ox, has four hooves. This made the order of the animals easy to remember, although it doesn't quite explain why these particular animals were chosen in the first place.

According to another theory, animals and their places in the order are explained by the correlation between their natural activities and certain times of the day or night. The Ten Celestial Stems and the Twelve Earthly Branches divide a day into twelve two-hour periods. To tell the time, you'd have to know, for example, that rats are probably most active between 11:00 p.m. and 1:00 a.m., that snakes (the sixth animal) begin to come out of their dens between 9:00 a.m. and 11:00 a.m., and that pigs aren't sleeping soundly until between 9:00 p.m. and 11:00 p.m.

The most fanciful explanation suggests that the Chinese zodiac originated in a race that was set up by the Jade Emperor, a legendary mythic and religious figure in Taoism. He invited every animal in existence to participate in the race, but only twelve showed up. The rat won, which is why it is first in the zodiac. The other animals are ordered according to how they finished in the race. The lumbering pig came in last.

Regardless of it origins, some people believe in the Chinese zodiac every bit as fiercely as others believe in the Western zodiac. And others say with a smirk that whether you think of yourself as a Snake or a Taurus, the whole thing should be taken with a grain of salt.

DO FARMERS REALLY NEED THAT EXTRA HOUR OF DAYLIGHT SAVING TIME?

Sure, go and blame farmers because you lose a whole hour of sleep every spring. It's a common misconception that Daylight Saving Time (DST) was created to help farmers. The truth is, they're none too pleased about it either. You see, cows and crops don't really care what the clock says. They're on "God's Time," otherwise known as Apparent Solar Time. When the sun's up, they're up. And when the clock is set an hour later, farmers lose a whole hour of morning productivity.

So if you can't point your tired little finger at the farmers, then who is responsible? Well, it was Benjamin Franklin who first proposed the idea of "saving daylight." While serving as the American delegate to France in 1784, he wrote an essay titled "An Economical Project for Diminishing the Cost of Light."

In it, the thrifty Franklin discussed resetting clocks to make the most use of natural daylight hours. This, he said, could save Parisian families "an immense sum" per year in the cost of tallow and wax for evening candles.

Though many were intrigued by Franklin's essay, the concept of daylight saving didn't take hold until more than a century later, when Englishman William Willett presented it again in his pamphlet "The Waste of Daylight" (1907). When World War I began, the British Parliament enacted DST throughout England to reduce the need for artificial lighting and save fuel.

In 1918 the U.S. Congress followed suit, placing America on DST to conserve resources for the remainder of the war. Even back then, DST was widely unpopular. The law was repealed in 1919 and not observed again until WWII, when President Roosevelt instituted year-round DST, called "War Time," from 1942 to 1945.

From 1945 to 1966 there were no U.S. laws regarding DST. This meant that states and local towns were free to observe DST—or not. How did anyone know what time *Bonanza* was on? Suffice it to say, there was plenty of confusion.

Congress took action in 1966, enacting the Uniform Time Act to establish consistent timelines across the country. But any area that wanted to remain exempt from DST could do so by passing a local ordinance.

The Energy Policy Act of 2005 extended DST, beginning in 2007, to the time it is currently: it begins at 2:00 a.m. on the second Sunday in March and ends at 2:00 a.m. on the first Sunday in November. Proponents of DST say that it saves energy and prevents traffic accidents and crimes while providing extra daylight time for outdoor activities. Still, DST has its share of detractors.

The farming state of Indiana—one of the last states to adopt statewide DST, in April 2006—has fueled the DST debate. A 2007 study by Matthew Kotchen and Laura Grant of the University of Santa Barbara concluded that enacting DST in Indiana actually increased electricity consumption in the state, costing Indiana households an additional $8.6 million in 2007.

So, does DST conserve energy, as was originally intended? Well, it seems that DST has us turning off the evening lights but cranking up the AC. Inventive as he was, Benjamin Franklin never foresaw that.

HOW LONG IS A DAY ON MARS?

The Martian solar day lasts about twenty-four hours and forty minutes. That's not much longer than a day on Earth, but it would give Earthlings who might eventually colonize the red planet a substantial advantage. Think about how much more you could accomplish with an extra forty minutes per day. It would amount to about an extra twenty hours per month, which ain't chump change.

Those colonists would need to adjust their calendars as well as their clocks. A year on Mars is about 687 Earth days. This is because Mars has a much longer path of orbit around the sun. Earth zips around the sun almost twice before Mars completes one full circuit.

Because of its extended path of orbit, Mars experiences four seasons that last twice as long as those on Earth. Spring and summer are almost two hundred days each; fall and winter are about one hundred fifty days each. Martian farmers would have a lot of time to plant and harvest, but they'd also have to conserve that harvest through a much longer and harsher winter.

Everything lasts longer on Mars than on Earth. For those colonists, the Martian work week would be an extra three hours and twenty minutes, and the weekend would be extended by an hour and twenty minutes. Summer vacation would be long, but the school year would be longer still.

A blessing or a curse? Depends on what you're doing with your extra forty minutes per day.

WHOSE GRANDFATHER IS THE GRANDFATHER CLOCK NAMED AFTER?

At first blush, the answer to this question seems obvious. Think about it: when's the last time you saw a grandfather clock in the house of a person under the age of sixty? Not for some time, if ever. Grandfather clocks—with their long cases, pendulums, echoing chimes, and Roman numerals—belong to the world of parlors, davenports, rose-water perfume, angel figurines, and cut-glass bowls filled with licorice candies that have been sitting out for decades. In short, the world of grandparents.

While this may seem like the obvious answer, the real reason these timekeeping devices—technically named "longcase clocks"—picked up the grandfatherly nickname has nothing to do with grandparents. However, it has everything to do with a song that your grandparents (or more likely your great-great-grandparents) might have heard when they were young.

In 1876, songsmith Henry Clay Work grew curious about a stopped longcase clock that stood in the foyer of the George Hotel in Piercebridge, England. The clock, the hotel's employees told him, was broken but was kept on the premises in memory of the Jenkins brothers, two longtime proprietors of the George. Seems the clock kept perfect time throughout their lives, but when the first Jenkins brother died, it started to falter. Soon after, the second brother died and the clock stopped altogether, despite the best efforts of a host of repairmen.

Work was struck by the story and wrote a ditty about the clock. In the song, the timepiece is referred to as "my grandfather's clock." The first verse goes something like this:

My grandfather's clock
Was too large for the shelf,
So it stood ninety years on the floor;
It was taller by half
Than the old man himself,
Though it weighed not a pennyweight more.
It was bought on the morn
Of the day that he was born,
And was always his treasure and pride;
But it stopped short
Never to go again,
When the old man died.

Okay, perhaps old H. C. wasn't Bob Dylan. But his song was an instant hit, and soon, most people had dropped the clunky term "longcase clock" for the hipper "grandfather clock."

With the advent of digital technology and atomic clocks, some clock lovers worry that the old pendulum-swinging grandfathers may not be long for the timekeeping world. However, despite its inanity, H. C. Work's song lives on. It was recorded multiple times in the twentieth century and as recently as 2004 by the R&B act Boys II Men. It's the song that keeps on ticking.

WHO CREATED TIME ZONES?

On a pleasant July evening in 1876, Sir Sanford Fleming was waiting in a railroad station in Bandoran, Ireland, for a train that had been listed in his *Railway Travelers Guide* as being due at 5:35. When the train failed to arrive, he inquired at the ticket office and learned that it stopped there at 5:35 in the morning, not 5:35 in the evening. Fleming might have just fired off an irritated letter to the editor of the *Guide*; instead, he decided it was time to change time.

Up to that point, the sun had ruled time. Earth rotates at approximately 17.36 miles per minute, which means that if you move thirty-five miles west of your present location, noon will arrive about two minutes earlier. Going the same distance east, it will come two minutes later. Confusing? Yes. But back in horse-and-buggy days, keeping precise track of time wasn't such an issue. What difference did a few minutes make when your only goal was to arrive at your destination before sundown?

The invention of the railroad altered this ancient perception of time forever. To run efficiently, railroads needed a schedule, and a schedule needed a timetable, and every minute did indeed count. Fleming, who had worked as a railroad surveyor in Canada, was more aware of the confusion over time than most people. Each railroad company used its own time, which was set according to noon at company headquarters. A weary traveler might be faced with five or six clocks at the station. Which one was correct?

Fleming came up with what he believed to be an ingenious solution. Earth would be divided into twenty-four sectors (like the sections of an orange), each consisting of fifteen degrees latitude. Each section would be a time zone, its clocks set exactly one hour earlier than the preceding zone.

Though Fleming's proposal was a model of common sense, he had a hard time convincing people to buy into it. The United States was an early adoptor, mandating four continental time zones in 1883. A year later, President Chester Arthur assembled the International Prime Meridian Conference in Washington, D.C. Twenty-five nations were invited and nineteen showed. They chose the Royal Observatory at Greenwich, England, as the Prime Meridian because it was already used by the British Navy to set time.

It wasn't until 1929, however, that standard time zones were instituted worldwide. Fleming also proposed the use of a twenty-four-hour clock, which would have meant that his evening train would have been scheduled to arrive at 17:35 rather than 5:35. This never caught on, except in the military and hospitals.

The sun remains our touchstone when it comes to time. We still recognize the twin poles of noon and midnight—one light, the other dark. Each, however, has the same number affixed to its name, which reminds us that on this planet, what goes around will always come around again.

HOW DID PEOPLE WAKE UP BEFORE ALARM CLOCKS?

Everyone has a trick for waking up on time. Some people put the alarm clock across the room so that they have to get out of bed to turn it off; some people wake up to the smell of the automatic coffeemaker; some set the clock ahead by ten or fifteen minutes to try to fool themselves into thinking that it's later than it really is; some even set multiple alarms or phone/alarm combos; and some—those boring Goody Two-Shoes types—simply go to bed at a reasonable hour and get a good night's sleep.

We don't necessarily rely on it every day, and some of us definitely don't obey it very often, but just about everybody has some kind of electronic device to help them get out of bed. How did anyone ever wake up before these modern marvels existed?

Many of the toughest problems in life have a common solution: hire someone else to do it. Long ago in England, you could hire a guy to come by each morning and, using a long wooden pole, knock on your bedroom window to wake you up so that you would get to work on time. This practice really took off during the Industrial Revolution of the late eighteenth century, when getting to work on time was a new and innovative idea. (In the grand tradition of British terminology that makes Americans snicker, the pole operator was known as a "knocker-up.") There's no word on how said pole operator managed to get himself up on time, but we can guess.

The truth is, you don't need any type of alarm to wake up, and you never did. Or so science tells us. Your body's circadian rhythms give you a sort of natural wake-up call via your body temperature's daily fluctuation. It rises every morning regardless of when you went to bed. Studies conducted at Harvard University seem to indicate that this rising temperature wakes us up (if the alarm hasn't already gone off).

Another study, conducted at the University of Lubeck in Germany, found that people have an innate ability to wake themselves up very early if they anticipate it beforehand. One night, the researchers told fifteen subjects that they would be awakened at 6:00 a.m. Around 4:30 a.m, the researchers noticed that the subjects began to experience a rise in the stress hormone adrenocorticotropin. On the other two nights, the subjects were told that they would get a 9:00 a.m. wake-up call but those diligent scientists shook them out of bed three hours early, at 6:00 a.m. And this time, the adrenocorticotropin levels of the subjects held steady in the early morning hours.

It seems, then, that humans relied on their bodies to rouse themselves from the dream world long before a knocker-up or an alarm clock ever existed.

WHO MADE GREENWICH, ENGLAND, THE WORLD'S OFFICIAL TIMEKEEPER?

Time Zones May Be Bewildering, but It Could Be Worse.

In fact, before 1884, it *was* worse. The rise of the railway system in the nineteenth century created the need for a more universal and precise timekeeping system. With every city keeping its own time, railroad companies were incapable of maintaining any semblance of a schedule, leading to utter havoc in rail travel: passengers missed trains or connections because their watches were set to different times than those of the railways. Nineteenth-century train stations were confused messes that resembled the way O'Hare International Airport looks today.

It became clear that something needed to be done. By the 1850s England's railways had standardized their times to London time, while France had standardized theirs to Rouen time. It was slightly more complicated in the United States, due to the nation's enormous latitudinal sprawl. But on November 18, 1883, the four time zones we Americans know and love went into effect, having been established earlier in the year by an association of railway operators that was called the General Time Convention.

This, however, didn't solve the problem of synchronizing global time. Consequently, the United States organized the International Meridian Conference in 1884, with the stated goal of selecting a global prime meridian and developing a standard "universal day." Delegates from more than two dozen countries attended the conference in Washington, D.C., and agreed that the Prime Meridian—the line at which longitude is considered to be zero degrees and is, thus, the starting point of world time—would pass through Greenwich, England.

Why Greenwich? For hundreds of years, Greenwich had been home to the Royal Observatory; its clock was the one London had used to officially set its time. By the mid-eighteen hundreds, all of the railways in England had set their timetables by Greenwich Mean Time; even before the aforementioned conference, time in England essentially had been standardized. After all, the sun had not yet set on the British Empire, and its enormous amount of international shipping was based on British-designed sea charts and schedules—charts that used Greenwich Mean Time as their foundation.

And for the rest of the world, it made sense to use a system that was already largely in place.

HOW LONG IS A NEW YORK MINUTE?

New Yorkers have a reputation for being rude, provincial, haughty, and hurried—and for good reason. They won't hesitate to tell you that there are no bagels like New York bagels, no delis like New York delis, no theaters like Broadway theaters, no avenues like Fifth Avenue, and no teams like the Yankees.

New Yorkers even seem to believe that their units of time are superior to the pedestrian measurements the rest of us use. Think a minute lasts sixty seconds? Not in New York.

Sometimes a minute can seem like a pretty long time. Try holding your breath for a minute. Or holding a sack of cement. Or speaking with a New Yorker. And sometimes the word "minute" merely signifies a short, indefinite period of time—consider how we use the word colloquially, as in, "I'll be back in a minute" or "I was into that band for, like, a minute." The phrase "New York minute" carries a similar meaning.

Ironically, it doesn't appear as if New Yorkers coined the phrase. According to most etymologists, it probably originated in Texas. The disdain of Texans for New Yorkers (or just about any city slickers) might be thinly masked, but "New York minute" isn't really that much of an insult.

In popular usage, it merely means a short unit of time, possibly playing on the idea that life in New York City is hectic and a minute in the hurried atmosphere of the Big Apple passes more quickly than in the rest of the world. How fast? Well, according to *The* (Galveston, Tex.) *Daily News*, where the phrase first appeared in print in 1954, a New York minute lasts about thirty seconds.

But a New York minute might be even shorter than that. As Johnny Carson once put it, a New York minute is the amount of time that lapses between the light changing to green and the jerk behind you starting to honk.

WHY DOES TIME SEEM TO MOVE FASTER AS YOU GET OLDER?

Many of the "benefits" of growing old seem to involve decreased speed. It takes longer to walk across the room because we're not as fleet of foot. We speak more slowly as our aged brains struggle to keep pace with our mouths. Amorous advances require a little more patience because of certain physiological transformations. And then there's the driving-slow-in-the-left-lane deal.

But nature appears to quicken one thing as we age: the passage of time. The older we get, the more often we find ourselves saying, "Really? That happened twelve years ago? I thought it was more like three years ago."

In 1975, University of Cincinnati professor Robert Lemlich published a paper on time perception. (We could swear it was more like 1988.) Working on the assumption that as a person ages, each year accounts for a smaller fraction of his or her entire life, Lemlich devised an equation comparing one year in the life of a forty-year-old to one year in the life of a ten-year-old. He concluded that time goes by twice as fast for the forty-year-old. To arrive at this finding, he divided ten years into forty, took the square root of that result, and ended up with the number two.

Got all that? We didn't, either. We just thought it necessary to include some math in the answer. But it's Lemlich's basic premise that's important: the longer you live, the shorter any given

increment of time seems relative to the length of your life. Time isn't moving faster, but your perception of time is changing.

Proof? When you're five, a year of kindergarten seems like an eternity. But when you're fifty, that annual prostate exam seems to come up about every six weeks.

HOW DID THE DAYS OF THE WEEK GET THEIR NAMES?

Just like our language itself, the English words for the days of the week have changed over time and embody a hodgepodge of unexpected influences. Some words came from the ancient Babylonians and some came from the Greeks and Romans. The rest were coined by the Anglo-Saxons, and you have our permission to blame these Germanic settlers of fifth-century Britain for all of the times that you misspelled "Wednesday" when you were a kid.

The Babylonians probably decided on a seven-day week because they were following the lunar cycle (about 29.5 days), and each phase of the lunar cycle lasts about seven days. They named the first day after the sun and the second after the moon. That's sensible enough. Enter the Romans. They retained the names of those first two days and followed the Babylonians' custom of naming days for heavenly bodies and their representative deities.

The Romans named the third day of the week for Mars, which was named after the god of war; the fourth for Mercury, god of merchants and messenger of the gods; the fifth for Jupiter, god of the sky, who brought rain and lightning; the sixth for Venus, goddess of love; and the last day of the week for Saturn, god of seed. The Romans then took along their calendar on a four-hundred-year visit with the inhabitants of England. And when the Romans finally skedaddled back to Italy, in barged the Anglo-Saxons.

The Anglo-Saxons were so occupied with carving out their own kingdoms on English soil that they found time to rename only four of the seven days—they retained the sun, moon, and Saturn monikers. For the rest, the Anglo-Saxons—like those before them—retained the celestial orientation and turned to their own gods. Interestingly, the Anglo-Saxons endeavored to correlate each of their gods with its Roman counterpart. So for the third day of the week, the Anglo-Saxons turned to Tiw, their version of the god of war. For the fourth day, they chose Woden, the closest thing to a supreme deity. The fifth day went to Thor, god of thunder. And the sixth was named for their god of love, Frigg. (Yes, we're serious—Frigg. This explains a few things about the Anglo-Saxons.)

Variant spellings evolved, but, basically, what the Anglo-Saxons called *sunnan daeg* is now Sunday. *Monan daeg* is now Monday. *Tiwes daeg* evolved into Tuesday. *Wodnes daeg* (which didn't evolve nearly enough) became Wednesday. *Thorsdagr* is Thursday. *Frigedaeg* is Friday. And *Saeterdag* is Saturday. And you now also have our permission to declare, "Thank Frigg it's Friday!"

1. How long was a week in Rome during the early days of the Roman Empire?
a. 5 days
b. 7 days
c. 8 days
d. 9 days

2. The Chinese calendar can have up to, but no more than:
a. 10 months
b. 12 months
c. 13 months
d. 15 months

3. How long is a fortnight?
a. 4 nights
b. 14 nights
c. 28 nights
d. 40 nights

4. The term for 1/100th of a second is:
a. A point
b. A jiffy
c. A cent
d. A willy milly

5. If you decide to rob a bank, statistically you're most likely to do it on this day.
a. Monday
b. Wednesday
c. Friday
d. Saturday

6. How long was a full day during the time of the dinosaurs?
a. The same as now
b. About 23 hours
c. About 12 hours
d. About 34 hours

7. How long does it take the Moon to orbit the Earth?
a. About 23 hours
b. About a week
c. About 23 days
d. About 27 days

8. Which of the following built a working pendulum clock?
a. Christiaan Huygens
b. Isaac Newton
c. Benjamin Banneker
d. John Harrison

9. When was the hourglass invented?
a. About 500 BC
b. About 250 BC
c. About 50 BC
d. About 25 BC

10. Clocks run clockwise because:
a. Ancient race courses ran in this direction.
b. No one is certain why.
c. That's the way the Earth moves around the Sun.
d. That's the way shadows move on sundials in the northern hemisphere.

1.
c. 8 days

2.
c. 13 months

3.
b. 14 nights

4.
b. A jiffy

5.
c. Friday

6.
b. About 23 hours

7.
d. About 27 days

8.
a. Christiaan Huygens

9.
b. About 250 BC

10.
d. That's the way shadows move on sundials in the northern hemisphere.

HUMAN BEINGS, REAL, IMAGINARY, AND OTHERWISE

At some point you figured out that Ronald McDonald wasn't real. But what about Orville Redenbacher? Grizzly Adams? With the sheer volume of media content we're assaulted with each day, it's no wonder if we're not always clear on where to draw the line between fact and fiction. The same confusion exists if you go back through history. Legends and tall tales have a habit of finding their way into biography and anecdote—and the other way around, too.

That bow-tied, popcorn-peddling snack fanatic? He was a real guy. And John "Grizzly" Adams (1812–1860) was more than a TV character—he was a real hunter who supplied bears to restaurants, zoos, and circuses.

WHO WAS OSCAR MAYER?

If you grew up in the 1960s or '70s, you probably knew the Oscar Mayer wiener jingle by heart. Now that you're older, you might think that Oscar—like Betty Crocker—was merely the invention of an advertising agency. Well, Ms. Crocker may be imaginary, but Mr. Mayer was a real person, and one with an inspiring Horatio Alger-esque story to boot.

Born in 1859 in Bavaria, Mayer came to the United States as a child. Eventually, in 1873, he made it to Detroit, where he spied a "help wanted" sign in the window of George Weber's meat market. Fourteen-year-old Oscar walked into the shop and took his first step toward realizing the American dream.

After working as Weber's "butcher boy" for a few years, Mayer decided to try his luck in Chicago, which was known at that time as "hog butcher for the world." He landed a job at Kohlhammer's meat market and later moved on to Armour & Co., where he worked for six years. After his brother Gottfried emigrated from Germany to join him, Oscar decided that it was time to go into business for himself.

The brothers rented a storefront on Chicago's north side. Gottfried was an expert *wurstmacher* (German for "sausage maker"), and Oscar knew how to run a business. Soon, a third brother—Max—joined the fledging company as a bookkeeper. People couldn't get enough of the Mayers' sausage—by 1900, they were making deliveries via horse and buggy throughout Chicago and to many surrounding towns.

Competition among butchers was fierce in those days. In 1904, fearing that imitators might damage their market's reputation, the Mayers took the novel step of branding their products. They used an image of edelweiss—an alpine flower that symbolizes purity. In fact, the Mayers were so convinced of their products' purity that they became one of the first companies to voluntarily submit to food safety inspections that were instituted in 1906.

Over the next two decades, the Mayers experimented with a variety of brand names, finally settling on "Oscar Mayer Wiener" in 1929. The name still appears on the company's packaging today. Oscar Mayer died in 1955 as a wealthy, successful, and beloved businessman.

The famous song made its debut several years later, in 1963. It still sometimes pops up on radio and TV, especially during baseball season. For those who don't want to wait to sing it again, here are the words:

Oh, I wish I were an Oscar Mayer wiener
That is what I'd truly like to be
'Cause if I were an Oscar Mayer wiener
Everyone would be in love with me!

WHO WAS SULEIMAN THE MAGNIFICENT?

And Just How Magnificent Was He?

He was a warrior-scholar who lived up to his billing. A Turkish Sultan who reigned from 1520–1566, Suleiman led the Ottoman Empire to its greatest heights. Not only was Suleiman a brilliant military strategist, he was also a great legislator, a fair ruler, and a devotee of the arts. During his rule, he expanded the country's military empire and brought cultural and architectural projects to new heights. For all this and more, Suleiman is considered one of the finest leaders of 16th-century Europe.

Under Suleiman's inspired leadership, his forces conquered Mesopotamia (now Iraq), and fended off the Safavid dynasty (modern Iran). The Ottomans would then successfully occupy Iraq until the First World War. Suleiman annexed or made allies of the Barbary Pirate states of North Africa, who remained a thorn in Europe's underbelly until the 1800s. He also led an army that went deep into Europe itself, crushing the Hungarian King Louis II at the great Battle of Mohács in 1526, which led to the Siege of Vienna.

An accomplished poet, Suleiman was gracious in victory, saying of the young Louis: "It was not my wish that he should be thus cut off while he scarcely tasted the sweets of life and royalty." To his favorite wife Hurrem, a harem woman and daughter of a Ukrainian Orthodox priest, he wrote: "My springtime, my merry faced love, my daytime, my sweetheart, laughing leaf . . . My woman of the beautiful hair, my love of the slanted brow, my love of eyes full of mischief."

While Shari'ah, or sacred law, ruled his farflung empire's religious life, Suleiman reformed the Ottomans' civil law code. In fact, the Ottomans called him Kanuni, or "The Lawgiver." The final form of Suleiman's legal code would remain in place for more than 300 years.

WHERE DID WE GET THESE CHARACTERS?

Who knows what makes some images endure while others slip through our consciousness quicker than 50 bucks in the gas tank. In any case, you'll be surprised to learn how some of our most endearing "friends" made their way into our lives.

The Aflac Duck

A duck pitching insurance? Art director Eric David stumbled upon the idea to use a web-footed mascot one day when he continuously uttered, "Aflac . . . Aflac . . . Aflac." It didn't take him long to realize how much the company's name sounded like a duck's quack. There are many fans of the campaign, but actor Ben Affleck is not one of them. Not surprisingly, he fields many comments that associate his name with the duck and is reportedly none too pleased.

Alfred E. Neuman, Mad Man

Chances are you're picturing a freckle-faced, jug-eared, gap-toothed kid, right? The character's likeness, created by portrait artist Norman Mingo, was first adopted by *Mad* in 1954 as a border on the cover. Two years later, the humor magazine used a full-size version of the image as a write-in candidate for the 1956 presidential election. Since then, several real people (for, um, various reasons) have been said to be "separated at birth" from Mr. Neuman, namely Ted Koppel, Jimmy Carter, and George W. Bush.

Betty Crocker

Thousands of letters were sent to General Mills in the 1920s, all asking for answers to all kinds of baking questions. Managers created a fictional character to give the responses a personal touch. The surname Crocker was chosen to honor a retired executive, and Betty was selected because it seemed "warm and friendly." In 1936, artist Neysa McMein blended the faces of several female employees to create a general likeness. Betty Crocker's face has changed many times over the years. She's been made to look younger, more professional, and most recently has a more multicultural look. At one point, a public opinion poll rating famous women placed Betty second to Eleanor Roosevelt.

Duke the Bush's Baked Beans Dog

Who else to trust with a secret recipe than the faithful family pooch? Bush Brothers & Company was founded by A. J. Bush and his two sons in 1908. A few generations later, the company is currently headed by A. J.'s grandson, Condon. In 1995, the advertising agency working for Bush's Baked Beans decided that Jay Bush (Condon's son) and his golden retriever, Duke, were the perfect team to represent the brand. The only problem was that the real Duke is camera shy, so a stunt double was hired to portray him and handle all the gigs on the road with Jay. In any case, both dogs have been sworn to secrecy.

The California Raisins

Sometimes advertising concepts can lead to marketing delirium (and vice versa). In 1987, a frustrated copywriter at Foote, Cone & Belding was working on the California Raisin Advisory

Board campaign and said, "We have tried everything but dancing raisins singing 'I Heard it Through the Grapevine.'" Somewhere a light bulb went off. With vocals by Buddy Miles and design by Michael Brunsfeld, the idea was pitched to the raisin folks. The characters plumped up the sales of raisins by 20 percent, and the rest is Claymation history!

Joe Camel

Looking for a way to revamp Camel's image from an "old man's cigarette" in the late 1980s, the R.J. Reynolds marketing team uncovered illustrations of Old Joe in their archives. (He was originally conceived for an ad campaign in France in the 1950s.) In 1991, the new Joe Camel angered children's advocacy groups when a study revealed that more kids under the age of eight recognized Joe Camel than Mickey Mouse or Fred Flintstone.

The Coppertone Girl

It was 1959 when a print ad for Coppertone first showed a suntanned little girl's white buttocks being exposed by a puppy. "Don't be a paleface!" was the slogan, and it underscored the commonly held belief of the time that a suntan was healthy. Artist Joyce Ballantyne Brand created the pig-tailed little girl from the image of her three-year-old daughter Cheri. When the campaign expanded from the printed page and into the world of television, it became Jodie Foster's acting debut. As the 21st century beckoned, and along with it changing views on sun exposure and child nudity, Coppertone revised the drawing to reveal only the girl's lower back.

Juan Valdez

This coffee lover and his trusty donkey have been ensuring quality coffee beans since 1959. Back then, the National Federation of Coffee Growers of Colombia wanted to give a face to the thousands of coffee growers in the industry. The Doyle Dane Bernback agency found one alright! By 1981, Valdez's image was so well known that it became part of the Federation's logo. Originally played by Jose Duval, the role was taken over by Carlos Sanchez from 1969 to 2006. In his spare time, Sanchez manages his own small coffee farm in Colombia.

The Gerber Baby

Contrary to some popular beliefs, it's not Humphrey Bogart, Elizabeth Taylor, or Bob Dole who so sweetly looks up from the label of Gerber products. In fact, the face that appears on all Gerber baby packaging belongs to mystery novelist Ann Turner Cook. In 1928, when Gerber began their search for a baby face to help promote their new brand of baby food, Dorothy Hope Smith submitted a simple charcoal sketch of the tot, promising to complete it if chosen. As it turned out, that wasn't necessary because the powers that be at Gerber liked it just the way it was. In 1996, Gerber updated its look, but the new label design still incorporates Cook's baby face.

Mr. Whipple

The expression "Do as I say, not as I do" took on a persona in the mid-1960s—Mr. Whipple, to be specific. This fussy supermarket manager (played by actor Dick Wilson) was famous for admonishing his shoppers by saying, "Ladies, please don't squeeze the Charmin!" The people at Benton & Bowles Advertising figured that if, on camera, Mr. Whipple was a habitual offender of his own rule, Charmin toilet paper would be considered the cushiest on the market. The campaign included a total of 504 ads and ran from 1965 until 1989, landing it a coveted spot in the *Guinness Book of World Records*. A 1979 poll listed Mr. Whipple as the third most recognized American behind Richard Nixon and Billy Graham.

The Pillsbury Doughboy

Who can resist poking the chubby belly of this giggling icon? This cheery little guy was "born" in 1965 when the Leo Burnett ad agency dreamt him up to help Pillsbury sell its refrigerated dinner rolls. The original vision was for an animated character, but agency producers borrowed a unique stop-action technique used on *The Dinah Shore Show*. After beating out more than 50 other actors, Paul Frees lent his voice to the Doughboy. So, if you ever craved Pillsbury rolls while watching *The Adventures of Rocky and Bullwinkle*, it's no wonder . . . Frees was also the voice for Boris Badenov and Dudley Do-Right.

Ronald McDonald

Perhaps the most recognizable advertising icon in the world, this beloved clown made his television debut in 1963, played by future *Today* weatherman Willard Scott. Nicknamed the "hamburger-happy clown," Ronald's look was a bit different back then: he had curly blond hair, a fast-food tray for a hat, a magic belt, and a paper cup for a nose. Ronald's makeover must have been a hit because today McDonald's serves more than 52 million customers a day around the globe.

WHO WAS THE REAL MCCOY?

This question doesn't have a definitive answer, although that hasn't stopped people from trying to find one. The phrase itself is invoked whenever a question of authenticity is raised. Given several options, the one true selection is referred to as "the real McCoy," meaning it is the genuine article and you should accept no substitute. But who is this McCoy fellow, and what makes him so real?

One of the most believable accounts involves a boxer who was active around the turn of the twentieth century. Norman Selby, who boxed under the name "Kid McCoy," was a frequent source of imitation, and it's said that he adopted the phrase "the Real McCoy" to distinguish himself from the drove of impostors.

Another explanation states that a brand of Scottish whiskey used the phrase as part of an advertising campaign, starting in 1870. G. Mackay & Co. Ltd. referred to itself as "the real Mackay," which is, of course, an alternate spelling (and pronunciation) of the now-popular idiom.

And then there's a theory that originates in the United States' prohibition period of the 1920s and 1930s. During this time, bootleg alcohol was quite a profitable business for those who weren't afraid to take some risks. It was even more profitable for the bootleggers who watered down their booze.

One man, however, wouldn't compromise the quality of the liquor he sold—you guessed it, a fellow named McCoy. Bill McCoy. He earned a hardy reputation by sailing between

Canada and the United States with contraband rum and whiskey on board. Shrewdly, McCoy dropped anchor in international waters (usually just outside Boston or New York City), where prohibition laws weren't in effect, and sold his wares legally to those who sailed out to him.

Although he might have made more money in the short term by watering down the booze he sold, McCoy was in it for the long haul and refused to taint his product. Therefore, the goods from his ship came to be known as "the real McCoy"—there was no diluted booze in McCoy's bottles.

So, who was the real McCoy? We may never know for sure. It appears there were several.

WHO WAS JERRY, AND WHY WAS HE SO GOOD AT RIGGING THINGS?

To be precise, Jerry never rigged any of those things; he built them. "Jerry-rig" is a confused conjoining of two separate and unequal phrases—"jury-rig" and "jerry-built"—and making the distinction is important if you want to keep your meaning clear/ not sound like an idiot.

The older of the two terms, "jury-rig," refers to a ship's mast. "Jury" is a nautical term for a replacement mast, while "rig" concerns the ropes, pulleys, sails, and other miscellany that make the ship go. Performing a jury-rig literally means replacing a broken mast with a new one.

The other phrase has less-definable origins. Some believe that it's a reference to the Biblical city of Jericho. The story goes that a group of soldiers knocked down the city's walls by circling it a number of times and blowing horns. Thus, a jerry-built structure is one that is prone to collapsing under very little strain.

The two phrases imply different levels of craftsmanship. A jury-rig is done at sea, sometimes in adverse conditions, and the replacement mast has to be good enough to get the crew home. It's not a task to be taken lightly. Jerry-built, on the other hand, refers to anything that's shoddily put together, using whatever tools and materials are handy. In nineteenth-century England, a jerry-builder was someone who constructed flimsy houses with cheap materials. Quick and dirty was the jerry-builder's way.

So it's really quite simple: jerry-built equals bad, jury-rig equals good. Confuse the two terms at your own peril.

WILL THE REAL HUMPTY DUMPTY PLEASE STAND UP?

Humpty Dumpty sat on a wall,
Humpty Dumpty had a great fall,
All the king's horses,
And all the king's men,
Couldn't put Humpty together again.

Fans of Lewis Carroll's *Alice's Adventures in Wonderland* and *Through the Looking Glass* will recall that Alice meets Humpty Dumpty during her adventures. In Carroll's tales, Humpty Dumpty is a giant egg with spindly legs and arms who waxes rhetorical about the meaning of "Jabberwocky." But the Humpty rhyme predates Carroll's stories by hundreds of years. Who was the original Humpty? And why is he depicted as an egg?

Nursery-rhyme scholars have several theories regarding the origin of the Humpty Dumpty nursery rhyme, which dates back to the fifteenth century, according to some estimates. The first candidate is Richard III, the Plantagenet king who was dumped from his horse at the Battle of Bosworth Field on August 22, 1485, and was promptly carved into pieces by his Tudor enemies. Shakespeare's depiction of Dick as a hunchback further supports the idea that he is the egghead featured in the rhyme. Unfortunately, there is no evidence anywhere outside of the Bard's imagination that Richard III had a hump on his back.

A second, more common explanation is that Humpty Dumpty refers not to a person but a thing—an enormous cannon. At the Battle of Colchester in 1648, during the English Civil War, a giant cannon was mounted atop a tower at St. Mary's by the Wall Church to defend the royalist stronghold from the upstart Roundheads, the Puritan supporters of Parliament. The tower was struck by Roundhead cannon fire and the great cannon plummeted to the ground, where it broke apart. Despite the best efforts of the king's horses and the king's men, nobody could put the cannon together again.

But the question remains: why is Humpty depicted as a giant egg? In the original print version, the Humpty rhyme doubled as a riddle. What object might fall and be unable to be put back together again? An egg, obviously. Well, perhaps it was obvious to people in the nineteenth century, when the rhyme first appeared in print. As for why Humpty would appear in Lewis

Carroll's stories to debate semantics with little Alice, we're not totally sure. But then, we could say that about most of the characters in Carroll's books.

WHO WAS SIMONYA POPOVA?

No one can accuse *Sports Illustrated* of not having a sense of humor. For laughs, it invented an attractive, camera-ready tennis star to rival Anna Kournikova. Her name was Simonya Popova. The September 2002 issue told of an unstoppable 17-year-old tennis force named Simonya Popova, a Russian from Uzbekistan and a media dream: 6'1", brilliant at the game, fluent in English, candid, busty, and blonde. She came from an appealing late-Soviet proletarian background and had a father who was often quoted in Russian-nuanced English. But she wouldn't be competing in the U.S. Open—her father forbade it until she turned 18.

The magazine verged on rhapsody as it compared Popova to Ashley Harkleroad, Daniela Hantuchová, Elena Dementieva, and Jelena Dokic. Editors claimed that, unlike Popova, all of these women were public-relations disappointments to both the Women's Tennis Association (WTA) and sports marketing because they chose to resist media intrusions to concentrate on playing good tennis. As a result, U.S. tennis boiled down to Venus and Serena Williams, trailed by a pack of hopefuls and won't-quite-get-theres. The gushing article concluded with this line: "If only she existed."

Just Kidding!

Popova *was* too good to be true. The biography was fiction, and her confident gaze simply showcased someone's digital artistry. Some people got it. Many didn't, including the media. They bombarded the WTA with calls: who was Popova and why wasn't she in the Open? The article emphasized what many thought—the WTA was desperate for the next young tennis beauty. WTA spokesperson Chris DeMaria called the story "misleading and irritating" and "disrespectful to the great players we have." Complaining that some people didn't read to the end of articles, he said, "We're a hot sport right now and we've never had to rely on good looks."

Sports Illustrated claimed it was all in grand fun. It hardly needed to add that it was indulging in puckish social commentary on the sexualization of women's tennis.

WHO WAS MONTEZUMA, AND WHY DID HE WANT REVENGE?

As Fred Willard's character puts it in the movie *Waiting for Guffman*, "Montezuma's revenge is nothing more than good old-fashioned American diarrhea. Adult diapers should never enter the picture." Specifically, Montezuma's Revenge is a general term for the kind of diarrhea that afflicts roughly half of the tourists who visit Mexico and Central America, and it's caused by contaminated food and water. While the locals aren't totally immune themselves, they have generally built up a better resistance to the disease-carrying microbes that are responsible for the runs.

The nickname, which became popular in the 1960s, refers to Montezuma II, a sixteenth-century Aztec emperor. From 1502 to 1520, Montezuma ruled the Aztec Empire in what is now southern Mexico, greatly expanding its reach and wealth by conquering other indigenous tribes. Everything was going swimmingly for Montezuma until the Spanish conquistador Hernán Cortés and his men showed up in 1519. According to some accounts, Montezuma and others believed that the Spaniards were gods whose coming was foretold by prophecy. But the Spaniards may have started this legend themselves after the fact. Anyway, Montezuma welcomed Cortés and his men as honored guests and showered them with gifts.

Before long, Cortés had set his sights on claiming the Aztec land and the civilization's considerable gold for Spain. His first step was to capture Montezuma and hold him as a sort of hostage. By manipulating Montezuma, Cortés attempted to subdue the Aztecs and persuade them not to resist the Spanish.

But many in the Aztec capital resented the Spanish and began to look down on Montezuma. When the Aztec people revolted against the conquistadors, Cortés commanded Montezuma to address the crowd and convince them to submit. Instead, they pelted Montezuma with stones. The emperor died three days later, though it's not clear whether the stoning was to blame or the Spanish executed him.

The revolt pushed the Spanish out of the capital. Eventually a new leader, Cuauhtemoc, sparked a revolt against Cortés. In the spring of 1521, the Spanish laid siege to the capital; Cuauhtemoc and his people surrendered a few months later. In just a few years, Cortés brought the Aztec Empire to an end.

So if the spirit of Montezuma is still lurking in Mexico, it makes sense that it might exact vengeance on foreign visitors. But if you're ever south of the border, it's best not to joke about Montezuma's revenge. Jimmy Carter made that mistake on an official visit in 1979, sparking a minor international incident that hurt already strained relations with Mexican President José López Portillo. President Carter didn't mean anything by the comment, but the reaction was understandable. What nation wants to be known for inducing mass diarrhea?

WHO WAS THE MODEL FOR THE STATUE OF LIBERTY?

For years, the first thing that immigrants saw when they arrived in America was the Statue of Liberty, which welcomed them from across New York's harbor. But who is she? Was she modeled after an actual woman, or was she simply a figment of sculptor Frédéric Auguste Bartholdi's imagination?

There are several women who may have been the original Miss Liberty, and not all of them were mortal. When Bartholdi accepted the commission to create a statue to honor the 1876 U.S. centennial, he may have turned to ancient history for his initial inspiration. The Romans personified liberty as the goddess Libertas, who was often depicted wearing flowing robes—just like America's Liberty. Historians have cited Libertas, who was embodied by a statue in the Roman Forum, as one potential prototype for Bartholdi's enormous lady.

Bartholdi, a Frenchman, may also have been inspired by his own country's icon of liberty. During the French Revolution, artists presented liberty in the guise of a beautiful woman named "Marianne." Today, you can see her holding a flowering branch aloft on a pedestal in front of the Place de la République in Paris. On a more earthly plane, Lady Liberty is said to bear a distinct resemblance to Isabella Eugenie Boyer, the French widow of a wealthy American entrepreneur, whom Bartholdi reputedly met through friends.

But goddesses and aristocrats seem to be odd models for the ultimate symbol of democracy. According to an article that appeared in *National Geographic* in 1986, Bartholdi may very well have found his inspiration far closer to home—in the face of his own mother, Charlotte Bartholdi, the woman who first encouraged him in his career. (From the neck down, the Geographic article claims, the statue was based on Bartholdi's mistress—later wife—Jeanne-Emile.)

So how does Lady Liberty measure up to our standards of beauty? The ancient Greeks used the golden ratio (or golden mean) to define the ideal proportions of everything from architecture to human beings. The ratio is about 1:1.618, so according to this formula, the perfect face should be 16.18 inches high if it is ten inches wide. Liberty's face measures approximately ten feet from ear to ear and seventeen feet, three inches from chin to crown, which results in a ratio of 1:1.73. Given her colossal size, that's almost spot-on.

Of course, Lady Liberty is more than just another pretty girl. She's the face of freedom, and is still beloved after all these years.

WHO WAS SARA LEE?

The advertising industry rakes in billions of dollars per year, and most of this success is based on one fact: people are gullible and easily manipulated. And they just love mascots. (How else does one explain the Taco Bell Chihuahua?) But we've got some bad news for those people: most mascots aren't real. A lot of the time, they're not even based on real people. The Morton salt girl? Nope. Aunt Jemima? Sorry. But what about Sara Lee, baker of various flavors of delicious cheesecakes that demand to be eaten in one sitting late at night in a dark room while you're depressed and watching paid programming? (Wait, that *is* normal, right?)

As it turns out, Sara Lee is a real person—but she was never a baker. The story of Sara Lee goes back to 1935, when Charles Lubin purchased a chain of three Chicago bakeries known as the Community Bake Shops. The popularity of the shops grew under Lubin's leadership, but it wasn't until 1949 that he hit upon the recipe that would make him rich.

That year, Lubin concocted a decadent cheesecake that was suited for freezing and selling in grocery stores. At his wife's behest, he named the product after his eight-year-old daughter, Sara Lee Lubin. The cheesecake proved to be enormously popular—so much so that a year later, Lubin renamed his company Kitchens of Sara Lee. In 1956 Lubin sold Kitchens of Sara Lee to Consolidated Foods, Inc., but by then, the Sara Lee cheesecake was so iconic that Consolidated Foods changed its name to the Sara Lee Corporation.

The original Kitchens of Sara Lee may be long gone, but Sara Lee herself is still alive—she is now known as Sara Lee Schupf. She never got into the baking game, but she certainly benefited from it: she was the sole heir to her father's fortune when he passed away in 1988. She became an active philanthropist—most notably supporting women in science—and a member of the American Academy of Arts and Sciences. So while the real Sara Lee may not be a baker, she has managed to make quite a mark on the world.

WHO IN THE SAM HILL WAS SAM HILL?

Colonel Samuel Hill made a bid for immortality, and depending on how you look at it, he either succeeded in spectacular fashion or failed miserably. His name is certainly remembered—often in times of frustration, bewilderment, and despair—especially if there happens to be a lady present.

"Sam Hill" has been used as a mild expletive, a replacement for "hell" or "damn," since at least the 1830s. The phrase was especially popular among cowboys, who used it in an attempt to clean up their language in mixed company. "Sam Hill" appeared in print for the first time in 1839, in the *Seattle Times*.

Several tales concerning the origin of this phrase have circulated throughout the years. One of them centers on Colonel Sam Hill, who hailed from Connecticut. Edwin Mitchell's *Encyclopedia of American Politics*, published in 1946, reports that the Colonel ran for political office repeatedly—and failed every time. Thus, to "go like Sam Hill" or to "run like Sam Hill" initially referred to Hill's relentless pursuit of office, even after it was obvious that the public did not want him there. Over time, the term devolved into the more general usage with which we are familiar today.

Another explanation is that "hill" is simply a sound-alike substitute for "hell," in the manner of "heck." It has been suggested that the name Sam comes from Samiel, the name given to the devil in Carl Maria von Weber's opera *Der Freischütz*. The opera was performed in New York City in 1825, a little more than a decade before the phrase's first print usage.

Still, for some, the name Sam Hill will always refer to the Colonel. He tried his hardest to make a place for himself in history and, in failing so many times, succeeded in a way he never could have imagined. No one remembers the man— Mitchell's entry is essentially the last remaining evidence of his existence—but we all know his name. Problem is, no one knows for sure what the Sam Hill it means.

WHO WAS KILROY?

Throughout World War II, graffiti that read "Kilroy was here" appeared everywhere—on ships, railroad cars, pavement, bunkers, fences, and any other surface that could hold a chalk mark. Alongside the slogan, there was usually a simple drawing of a face peering over a wall (presumably, Kilroy himself). So who was this Kilroy? And what was he doing here, anyway?

A definitive answer is elusive, but that hasn't stopped people from trying to find out. In 1946, just after the war ended, the American Transit Association offered a real trolley car to the real Kilroy. Approximately forty men tried to claim the prize, which was eventually awarded to forty-six-year-old James J. Kilroy of Halifax, Massachusetts. The judges thought that his story was the most convincing—we'll let you judge for yourself. During the war, Kilroy was an inspector at the Bethlehem Steel Shipyard in Quincy, Massachusetts, a yard that produced ships for the military effort. Kilroy discovered that he was being asked to inspect the same ship bottoms and tanks again and again, so he devised a way to keep track of his work: he used a yellow crayon to write "Kilroy was here" in big block letters on the hatches and surfaces of the ships he inspected.

Those ships went overseas with Kilroy's inscriptions intact. And over the course of the war, fourteen thousand shipyard employees enlisted, most of whom went overseas, too. No one knows who first decided to imitate the crayon-scrawled words, but before long, soldiers saw them everywhere they went. It became common practice for the first soldier into a new area to pull out a piece of chalk and let those behind him know that Kilroy had been there, too. But no soldier ever admitted to being the one who first wrote the words.

The accompanying illustration is even more mysterious. One theory suggests that it may have been adapted from a British cartoon character called Mr. Chad, who was always looking over a fence and saying, "Wot, no engine?" or "Wot, no tea?"

True or not, James J. Kilroy's story convinced the contest judges, and he won the trolley car. What did he do with it? Kilroy had a big family, so he attached the fifty-foot-long, twelve-ton trolley to his house and used it as a bedroom for six of his nine children.

WHO WAS DR. SEUSS AND DID HE EVER PRACTICE MEDICINE?

Written with just fifty different words, Dr. Seuss's *Green Eggs and Ham* is so succinct that it could have been scrawled on a prescription pad. But the only medicine that this "doctor" ever prescribed was humor, whimsy, and perhaps a side of one fish two fish red fish blue fish.

Born on March 2, 1904, in Springfield, Massachusetts, Dr. Seuss was the son of a brewmaster father and a pie-baker mother. His given name was Theodor Seuss Geisel. (Seuss was his mother's maiden name.) So how did Theodor go from being a simple "Ted" to the world's most famous "doctor" of children's art and literature?

The story begins when Ted was a student at Dartmouth College. In the spring of 1925, he was the editor-in-chief of the university's humor magazine, *Jack-O-Lantern*. Unfortunately, his editorial tenure was cut short after he and his friends got caught throwing a party that featured gin. These, remember, were the days of Prohibition. But getting fired from his position didn't stop Ted from dispensing his occasional dose of drollery—he continued to write for and contribute cartoons to *Jack-O-Lantern*. To elude punishment, he signed his work with clever pseudonyms like "L. Pasteur," "L. Burbank," "D. G. Rossetti," and his middle name: "Seuss."

Seuss took on the self-appointed title of "doctor" several years later when he published his first children's book, *And to Think That I Saw It on Mulberry Street*, in 1937. It's said that he added the mock-scholarly "Dr." to his name as a joke. You see, Seuss's father had always wanted him to earn a doctorate and become a professor—and that didn't exactly happen. Seuss did go on to study at Oxford University in England after graduating from Dartmouth, but he became bored with academics and ditched his studies for a tour of Europe instead.

Back to that very first book: though it's hard to imagine, success as an author and illustrator was slow for the young doc. *Mulberry Street* was rejected by multiple publishers before it was finally released by Vanguard Press. Of course, once printed, the book won much praise for its unique illustrations. After that, a string of wildly popular works followed.

At the time of his death in 1991, Dr. Seuss had published nearly fifty books—including the classics *Horton Hears a Who* (1954), *The Cat in the Hat* (1957), *Fox in Socks* (1965), *The Lorax* (1971), and *Oh, the Places You'll Go!* (1990)—and he's sold more books than any other American children's author. He's also won two Academy Awards, two Emmy Awards, a Peabody Award, and the Pulitzer Prize.

But guess what? According to Theodor's widow, Audrey Geisel, Seuss didn't much like to spend time with children. He never had any of his own and, in fact, was "afraid of children to a degree." Good thing the doctor didn't become a pediatrician!

WHO WAS THE ORIGINAL PIED PIPER?

"The Pied Piper of Hamelin" is one of the most popular folktales in the world—it's estimated that it's known by more than one billion people. It's also one of the creepiest. This is not

only because it's a mysterious tale of disappearing children—
it's because the villain of the story, the Piper, is described as
wearing "motley clothing of many colors." There are some
things that are just plain scary, and a stranger wearing pied garb
and playing a flute in the streets of your town is one of them.
But just who this transient flautist actually was is up for debate.

For those of us who have forgotten our German folklore, the
story of the Pied Piper of Hamelin goes a little something like
this. Back in 1284, the village of Hamelin was overrun by rats.
Just as the villagers were reaching their wits' ends with the
vermin, a stranger appeared in town, dressed in multi-colored
("pied") garb and carrying a pipe.

The stranger promised the villagers that he would rid the town
of its rats for a fee. After the deal was struck, he played his
pipe and lured the rats into the river. The Hamelinites, though,
refused to pay the Piper his due. It was a decision that they
would rue, for a short time later the Piper returned. He played
his mysterious music and lured all 130 children of the town into
the mountains, where they disappeared into a cave, never to be
heard from again. Creepy. But also remarkable, especially when
one considers that the story of the Pied Piper of Hamelin, unlike
most folktales, has specific dates and numbers attached to it.
This has led some scholars to conclude that the tale is based on
actual events—indeed, it has been suggested that the Piper was,
in fact, a notorious child-killer who rampaged through Hamelin
in the late thirteenth century. However, there's no written
evidence of such crimes, and the story—despite the fact that it
contains uncommon detail—is actually very similar to folktales
about rat-killing, child-luring musicians that have been told in
other countries. This theory, then, is probably untrue.

Another explanation asserts that the tale may be an allegory, perhaps of the Black Death—which swept the land during the mid-fourteenth century—or, more likely, of colonization. At around the end of the thirteenth century, Germany was expanding, settling the lands near its eastern borders in what is today Poland, Romania, and the Czech Republic. Settlement recruiters wandered the German countryside to gather volunteers for new settlements from the rural poor. At this time, Germany wasn't a very nice place, and after the Black Death took hold, it became even less pleasant. It didn't take much to convince the region's youth to seek greener pastures out east.

This theory gained major currency when a German linguist studied the surnames of families in Polish settlements that were founded around that time. To his surprise, he discovered that the names in some of the cities and towns were very similar to those found in the area of thirteenth-century Hamelin, which led him to suggest that a mass exodus from Hamelin during the time frame in question may have spawned the Pied Piper tale.

So, ultimately, the Pied Piper was probably not based on a real person. Nonetheless, if you happen to come across a motley-clad man playing a flute in your neighborhood, it's probably wise to avoid him.

WAS THERE A REAL JOHN DOE?

There is no single John Doe from whom the rest have followed. The name is today what it has always been: a placeholder. John Doe is used when a person's name is unknown or when a person wishes to remain anonymous. It first appeared in legal proceedings known as "actions of ejectment," which were common in England from medieval times until 1852 and were also used in the United States. In these proceedings, John Doe was the fictional name for the plaintiff; the name substituted for the defendant was the equally fictional Richard Roe.

An action of ejectment could be brought to the court by a person who had been thrown out of his own property by a trespasser or who had rented his property to a tenant who stopped paying rent and refused to leave. Either way, the person occupying the property had no right to be there, and the owner wanted him out.

Enter John Doe and Richard Roe. The property owner claimed in court to have granted a lease to John Doe; John Doe, in turn, claimed to have been kept from using the property by Richard Roe. A letter was then sent to Richard Roe, urging him to appear in court. Because there wasn't a Richard Roe, the real-life defendant came to the court to speak on his own behalf. The court allowed this, at which point the fictional lease became moot and the subject turned to the ownership of the land's title.

Is your head spinning yet? The process was overly complex, and it's anyone's guess why a person couldn't use his own name to argue property issues. England's Common Law Procedure Act, which was passed in 1852, did away with the action of ejectment and streamlined eviction proceedings. American law, however, continued the practice well into the twentieth century, using the same proxies for actual citizens.

Who came up with these names? It is likely that John and Richard were chosen because they were common names. The origins of Doe and Roe are murkier. They might refer to deer: a doe is a female deer, and a roe is a type of deer native to Europe.

Or they might have been chosen because one indicates deer and the other fish ("roe" can also refer to a mass of fish eggs), the thought process being that both deer and fish were commonly poached. Either way, their origins seem to be as anonymous as the names themselves.

OSCAR WHO?

Every year, film buffs and celebrity oglers around the world tune in to watch the Academy of Motion Picture Arts and Sciences hand out its Academy Awards of Merit. But why are they referred to as "Oscars"?

The epic films *Ben-Hur* (1959), *Titanic* (1997), and *The Lord of the Rings: The Return of the King* (2003) each won 11 of them. The legendary Katharine Hepburn set the standard for professional acting, having won a record four of them in the category of Best Actress. Renowned British actor Peter O'Toole was nominated for eight over the course of his career, only to go home empty-handed every time."Them," of course, refers to the Academy Awards of Merit, the illustrious prizes handed out annually by the Academy of Motion Picture Arts and Sciences for excellence in the fields of movie acting, writing, directing, producing, and technology.

The eight-and-a-half-pound gold-plated statuette that symbolizes the epitome of film industry success is formally called the Academy Award of Merit, or the Academy Award, for short. So, how is it that the award became known as "Oscar"?

Credit for originating the name is generally given to former Academy executive director Margaret Herrick. In 1931, as a librarian with the Academy, Herrick remarked that the statuette's art-deco figure reminded her of her Uncle Oscar. The name stuck, and in 1939 the Academy began using both "the Academy Award" and "the Oscar" as the official tag of its prized prize.

WHO WAS DAVY CROCKETT?

Well, he was a man from Tennessee—that much is for sure. Some aspects of David "Davy" Crockett's life are not in dispute, though much of it is. We know that he was born on August 17, 1786, in eastern Tennessee. His first wife was Mary "Polly" Finley, who died in 1815. He soon remarried, taking the widow Elizabeth Patton to be his bride. Crockett was an excellent hunter. Often his rifle enabled him to provide food for his wife and five children. But he wasn't entirely an outdoorsman: he was elected to the Tennessee legislature in 1821, then the United States House of Representatives in 1827. For the next decade he was in and out of Congress, and when he found himself in a hard-fought battle for the Congressional seat in 1835, he threatened that if he lost the election he would tell his constituents "to go to hell" and move to Texas. He lost the vote and kept his word, departing to Texas, where he met his end at the Alamo on March 6, 1836.

Two Men the Same—Two Men Different

Crockett is always lumped together with Daniel Boone as one of the two premier American frontiersmen, blazing trails through untamed wilderness. Without question, Boone was the real deal.

He explored the Kentucky and Tennessee regions when they were populated almost primarily by Native Americans, built the Wilderness Road to provide settlers with greater access to the new lands, personally led settlers into Kentucky when it was just a howling wilderness, and narrowly escaped death numerous times.

Crockett's life followed a different trajectory. Bitten by the political bug upon his first foray into elected office, he progressed from justice of the peace to U.S. Congressman in a remarkably short time, particularly because political campaigns then—as now—cost money, and Crockett's low-budget campaigns would have embarrassed a shoestring.

Crockett had a natural aptitude for politics and political shenanigans. He was independent-minded and loyal to his backwoods constituents. He was also gregarious, personable, and very quick-witted. Once, a large flock of boisterous guinea hens showed up at an outdoors political debate and squawked so loudly that his opponent was completely unnerved. Crockett, however, explained that the birds had actually been chanting "Crockett, Crockett, Crockett," which is why the other candidate was spooked. He won the debate and the election.

Contrast that with the stoic and reclusive Boone, who probably would have preferred to swim the entire length of the Mississippi River rather than hobnob and glad-hand voters. As one story has it, Boone once welcomed a visitor to his cabin and in conversation asked where the man lived. When informed that he resided about 70 miles from Boone's home, Boone turned to his wife and said, "Old woman, we must move, they are crowding us."

A Combustible Lion with a Touch of Airth-Quake

Congressman Crockett enjoyed using his reputation as a humble backwoodsman in sophisticated Washington, D.C. This reputation was spread even further by the incredibly popular 1831 play *The Lion of the West*. The main protagonist, obviously based on Crockett, is a Congressman from Kentucky named Nimrod Wildfire, who at one point boasts that he's "half horse, half alligator, a touch of the airth-quake, with a sprinkling of the steamboat." Beginning in 1835, with the publication of the so-called *Crockett Almanacs*, he was portrayed in an even more inflammatory light—as biographer Mark Derr calls him, a "comic Hercules."

Thanks to Walt Disney's glowing treatment in the mid-1950s, Davy Crockett became one of the first media sensations of the modern age. By the time Disney was finished with his legend, people everywhere were singing about Tennessee mountaintops and wearing coonskin caps (which, by the way, Crockett never wore). From then on, Crockett's image as an authentic American hero was set.

A Little of This, a Little of That

So who was Davy Crockett? Like all of us, he's hard to pin down—a combination of different factors that make a characterization difficult. Part frontiersman and part politician mixed with a lively wit and a friendly nature, Davy Crockett in the end was 100 percent uniquely American.

1. This folk hero was said to have beaten a steam machine in a rock-crushing contest.
a. Daniel Boone
b. Casey Jones
c. John Henry
d. Jumbo Reilly

2. Where did the Dolly Madison bakery brand get its name?
a. From a folk heroine known for her great baking skills
b. From a famous Philadelphia baker
c. From an infamous Philadelphia salon hostess
d. From the wife of U.S. president James Madison

3. All of the following pirates actually existed except:
a. Blackbeard
b. Calico Jack
c. Henry Morgan
d. Long John Silver

4. What was the real name of writer Lewis Carroll?
a. Donald Littlefield Chesterton
b. Charles Lutwidge Dodgson
c. Ludwig Donald Charleson
d. Luther Charles Carlson

5. Who was Guy Fawkes?
a. A fictional character who tried to assassinate an English king
b. An actual person who tried to blow up the English House of Lords
c. A Shakespearean character representing anarchy
d. An actual person who tried to become king of England

6. The Caesar salad is named after this person.
a. The chef Caesar Cardini
b. The Roman general Julius Caesar
c. The entertainer Cesar Romero
d. The Roman emperor Caesar Augustus

7. Does the song "John Jacob Jingleheimer Schmidt" refer to a real person?
a. Yes. He was a nineteenth-century German-American songwriter.
b. Yes. He was the son of Irving Berlin.
c. No. The name refers to a character in Boy Scout literature.
d. No. The origin of the name is unknown.

8. All of the following American outlaws actually existed except:
a. Josey Wales
b. Billy the Kid
c. Jesse James
d. William Quantrill

9. What was the real name of gangster Dutch Schultz?
a. Anselmo Luciano
b. Louis Schmierer
c. Ronald Schlatz
d. Arthur Flegenheimer

10. Who was Paul Bunyan?
a. A real person
b. A character originating in a play
c. A fictional character from folklore
d. A lumber industry marketing invention

1.

c. John Henry

2.

d. From the wife of U.S. president James Madison

3.

d. Long John Silver

4.

b. Charles Lutwidge Dodgson

5.

b. An actual person who tried to blow up the English House of Lords

6.

a. The chef Caesar Cardini

7.

d. No. The origin of the name is unknown.

8.

a. Josey Wales

9.

d. Arthur Flegenheimer

10.

c. A fictional character from folklore

WHAT'S THE DIFFERENCE BETWEEN A SAXOPHONE AND A CHAINSAW?

It's all in the grip. Ha cha cha! Imagine the mental state of inventor Adolphe Sax, as he sat brooding in his workshop. "My next instrument must be capable of great emotional range, with a liquid tone both earthy and ethereal," he must have thought. "But in the hands of a beginner, it should sound like a terrified piglet. Why? Because I am an evil man." Sax must have been unwell. Anyone who has lived with a budding saxophonist understands our sentiments.

HOW DID MUSIC BEGIN?

Skin, Bone, Rock, and Wood

In 2008, an ancient flute was found at Hohle Fels, a Stone Age cave in southern Germany. Nearly 40,000 years old, it could be the oldest musical instrument ever found. The flute was carved from the hollow wing bone of a vulture. It has five precisely chiseled finger holes and a V-shaped mouthpiece. Nobody can say for sure how it was used, or what Stone Age people thought about music. But music could have helped ancient humans build their society.

Before humans were making flutes, they were probably using their voices to mimic the sounds they heard around them. People have always enjoyed imitating the sounds of nature, so it is easy to imagine them mimicking insect sounds, whistling bird calls, or howling like wolves. While prehistoric musicians were busy showing off their vocal skills, they were also beginning to invent tools. As they pounded rocks into cutting edges, shaped branches into spears, and scraped animal skins, they may have noticed how pleasing the sounds they made were. Or perhaps it was just the younger, more excitable ones that were pleased with these sounds. The older ones may have already been griping about this newfangled rock 'n' scrape music.

The era of prehistoric music lasted from about 50,000 to 4000 BC. There is not much physical evidence of musical instruments from that time, but we know that by the time history was being written down, music was a big part of human culture.

Prehistoric musicians all made instruments from the building blocks they found in the natural world. In addition to the human voice, they created four basic types of musical instrument.

Aerophones

Aerophones make sound by vibrating air. An aerophone can be as simple as a whip cracking in the air. It can also be something made from wood or animal bone (like the 40,000-year old flute). You can hear the sounds of modern aerophones when a person blows into a bugle's mouthpiece, across a flute's edge, or over the reed of a saxophone.

Chordophones

Chordophones have strings stretched between two points. These strings were first made from plant fibers or animal gut. Plucking the strings caused them to vibrate. An early example is a simple harp: one string tied between two ends of a curved branch. It's easy to imagine the first chordophone being the string on a hunter's bow.

Membranophones

These are simply hollow cylinders that have membranes stretched tightly across them. Bass drums, snare drums, bongos, and many other types of drum belong to this family. 4,000 years ago, membranophones were made by stretching animal skin over a wooden frame, such as a hollow log. Some are still made this way. Today we make sounds with membranophones the same way ancient people did: by hitting the instrument with our hands or sticks.

Idiophones

Idiophones vibrate something other than air, strings, or membranes. Examples are stones, blocks of wood, triangles, chimes, gongs, and rattles. Stone Age Africans may have used stones as musical instruments two million years ago.

The Music of Early Civilization

The advanced society that arose in the land of Sumer was one of the first to have its own professional musicians. Starting around 5000 BC, Sumer's farmers began growing crops year-round. Abundant food led to the formation of cities and specialized jobs. Sumerian musicians played in the temple to honor the goddess Innanna. They performed for special occasions such as royal marriages and births. These were serious responsibilities, and the musicians would always wash their hands and heads before playing string instruments.

In ancient Egypt, musicians played at festivals, temples, palaces, farms, battles, and burials. Music was everywhere. Workers sang while grinding corn. Songs expressed love, praised the pharaohs, and honored Hathor, goddess of music, song, and dance. Many ancient Egyptian musical instruments were decorated with geometrical or flowery designs. Egyptians made many kinds of rattles, drums, cymbals, castanets, tambourines, and bells.

Musicians used hair or plant fiber for string instruments. They played wind instruments similar to flutes and oboes. They used reeds to construct primitive trumpets. Later, horn instruments were constructed from bronze and silver.

The word music itself comes from the ancient Greek word "muse" (a spirit who inspires literature, art, and knowledge). Music was a big part of life for Greeks, and many ordinary people could play an instrument. Music was heard at weddings, religious festivals, funerals, and concerts. In the fields, shepherds played pipes to calm their animals. In war, marchers and ships' oarsmen kept time to a drum. The child who grew up to be Alexander the Great even learned to play the lyre.

WHERE DID THE CLARINET COME FROM?

The first clarinet can be traced back to an invention by German instrument maker, Johann Christoph Denner, in the late 1600s. His early version of the clarinet looked like a recorder, but was made in three parts and had two additional keys close to the holes. The early clarinet had a piercing tone that was capable of being heard in large orchestras. It was also useful to orchestras because it could play loud or soft, or fast or slow. In 1791, Mozart composed a concerto specifically for the clarinet, and this helped promote the clarinet's reputation as a solo instrument. Early clarinets were made of boxwood, pear, or plum wood. The clarinet continued to evolve through the nineteenth century.

The modern clarinet is a thin tube made of either plastic or a heavy wood known as grenadilla. It has 18 holes in the tube. Padded metal keys cover 12 holes. The other six are covered (or uncovered) by the player's fingers. There's a mouthpiece at the top and a flared bell at the bottom. A single reed is attached to the bottom of the mouthpiece. When air passes across the reed, the vibration creates sound. When played, the clarinet is held straight up and down. The bottom lip is folded over the bottom teeth, the mouthpiece is held in the mouth, and the musician blows air through the opening. The word itself was coined from Italian words joined together to mean "little trumpet." Early clarinets were capable of playing high notes that had a shrill, brassy tone.

Early forms of the bass clarinet were developed in the eighteenth century. At that time, they were only used in orchestras. By the 1920s, bass clarinets were showing up in marching bands and other genres of music. The modern bass clarinet is also a single reed instrument. It has a range one octave lower than the regular clarinet, and is most common in classical orchestras. It has a warm, rich tone. Because of its weight, musicians usually attach it to a neck strap.

WHO WAS MARIA CALLAS?

In the history of modern opera, there have been a handful of legendary performers even non-opera fans can name drop, such as Luciano Pavarotti or Plácido Domingo. But perhaps the most famous name of them all is Maria Callas. Little Maria Anna Sophie Cecilia Kalogeropoulos was born in 1923 to unhappily married Greek immigrant parents. It was also around this time that the family's name was changed from Kalogeropoulos to the less unwieldy Callas.

Maria's mother, Evangelia, was a domineering and ambitious woman. When she learned that her chubby youngest daughter, Maria, could sing—and we mean *really* sing—she packed up her two daughters and returned to Athens (sans husband).

There, Evangelia hoped to enroll Maria at the famous Athens Conservatoire. Maria wasn't accepted, but she continued to train. She eventually landed a spot at the Conservatoire, wowing the admissions committee with her powerhouse style.

Hardest Working Diva in the Business

Under the tutelage of tough but encouraging teachers, Callas devoured librettos and scores for ten hours a day, not only learning her parts but the parts of the other singers, too. But this wasn't entirely because of her insatiable interest in music—she was myopic and seeing the conductor was difficult (and glasses definitely were not considered an option). In order to be able to follow along and not miss a beat, Callas had to know all the parts of every opera in which she took part.

In 1940, Callas signed on at the Greek National Opera. Two years later, the rising star landed a principal part in Eugen d'Albert's *Tiefland*. Reviewers and audiences were unanimous: Maria Callas was unlike anything they had ever seen. The emotion she brought to the roles she played was raw and real—a powerful combo of virtuoso voice and an extraordinary actress.

A Rise to Fame, Fortune—and Drama

By the time she left Greece in 1945 at the tender age of 21, Callas had given 56 performances in seven operas and had appeared in 20 recitals. Her teachers advised her to make a name in Italy first, then the center of the opera world. After making a short detour to the Metropolitan Opera in New York, she was under the guidance of Tullio Serafin, a maestro opera conductor whom Callas credited with launching her career. What was particularly amazing about her voice was her ability to sing dark, heavy roles and then jump to roles written for light, agile sopranos. Callas's abilities redefined the very concept of vocal range.

Her big break came when she stepped in as a replacement for another singer who fell ill before the opening of *I Puritani* in Venice. Never mind that she only had six days to learn the part and that she was already singing the large role of Brunnhilde in *Die Walkure*. It was a challenge she couldn't refuse.

Diets, Rumors, Heartbreak

Throughout the '50s, Callas dominated the Italian opera world, essentially launched the Chicago Lyric Opera with an inaugural performance of the lead in *Norma*, gave star turns in London, and was on the cover of *Time*. But with increased exposure came more backlashes against her. She had always been a robust woman, but then she lost about 80 pounds mid-career. Rumors circulated that she had taken a tapeworm pill. There were stories of diva behavior after a string of cancelled performances, lawsuits, and contract troubles. True, Callas was a force to be reckoned with, but those close to her knew that many of the stories had been either embellished or totally fabricated.

Whether it was the stress of being the world's most famous opera singer, the weight loss (some believed the diet contributed to her vocal decline), or simply the inevitable march of time, Callas's voice began to lose some of its luster throughout the '60s. Romantically, she had long been involved with shipping magnate Aristotle Onassis—she had left her husband for him in 1959—but when Onassis moved on to Jackie Kennedy, Callas was devastated.

In 1977, at age 53, Maria died in Paris of a heart attack. Since then, she's been named the greatest soprano of all time by the BBC, won a Grammy Lifetime Achievement Award, and her name still plays on the lips of anyone who is asked to name history's opera legends.

HOW DID WE GET THE BLUES?

Rural African Americans built the blues upon a tradition of spirituals and work songs that went back to the early days of slavery. Poverty, bad luck, love gone wrong—these were the themes of early blues songs. Yet the blues was more than lyrics about the dark side of life. The notes themselves had a way of emphasizing the point.

The Blue Note

Most blues songs deliberately change the notes in the major scale to create a specific mood. The third, fifth, and seventh notes can be flatted to give songs a powerful emotional flavor. These *blue notes* are so effective that they have found their way into many other modern forms, like jazz, rock, and country.

It may sound loose, but the blues actually follows strict rules. The most well-known of these is the *blues progression*. This refers to the chord structure of the song. A blues progression is typically divided into 12 measures (or bars) of three four-bar segments. This progression is usually in a 4/4 time signature. If you know the 12-bar blues progression, you can play hundreds of blues songs.

Call and Response

Early work songs often featured a solo singer
"calling" the first line of a melody and a group
chorus singing a response. This structure found
its way into the blues. As the guitar became
popular with African American musicians,
they used it to respond to their own vocals.

Blues in Transition

As African Americans left the South in the early twentieth
century in search of new opportunities, so did the blues. The
country blues of the Mississippi delta found its way to Texas
and other parts of the South, and spread north to cities like
Memphis, St. Louis, Chicago, and Detroit. The classic blues
style of the 1920s often featured female singers. Mamie Smith,
Ma Rainey, and Bessie Smith were some of the most popular
performers of this decade.

Shortly after WWII, the appearance of electric instruments
permanently changed the blues. Blues guitarists could now
plug into amplifiers and be heard over crowds in noisy bars.
In Chicago, musicians like Muddy Waters, Little Walter, and
Howlin' Wolf found that the electric sound could give the
blues a bold, urban edge. The rough, electric blues of Chicago,
Memphis, and other cities was the bedrock on which many later
American musical styles would be built.

WHERE DID THE BATON COME FROM?

It begins with a tragedy involving 17th-century composer Jean-Baptiste Lully. One day Lully was conducting his beautiful music at a rehearsal. As always, he was keeping time with a huge wooden staff that he pounded on the floor. On this fateful day, however, Lully missed the floor and drove the staff right into his foot.

No, this is not the moment the conductor's baton was conceived. Lully did not have an epiphany and say, "You know, I should use something smaller to direct my music." Nevertheless, the moment remains part of music history. An abscess developed on Lully's right foot that turned to gangrene. The composer did not have the foot amputated, causing the gangrene to spread and eventually leading to his death. And there you have it—a conducting fatality!

The Birth of the Baton

So when did conductors trade in those clumsy and potentially lethal wooden staffs for the symbolically powerful batons? And do they really need them? Don't a conductor's hands contain ten God-given batons?

Some conductors today use their hands and fingers, but most have a baton that they move to the music. The theory is that the baton—usually ten to twenty-four inches long and made of wood, fiberglass, or carbon—magnifies a conductor's patterns and gestures, making them clearer for the orchestra or ensemble.

Orchestras date to the late 16th century during the Baroque period, and conductors back then used the same type of staff that felled Lully. Sometimes there was no conductor at all. Instead, the leader was most often a keyboardist, who would guide the orchestra with gestures when his hands were free, or a violinist, who would set the tempo and give directions by beating the neck of his instrument or making movements with his bow. At other times, the keyboardist or violinist simply played louder so the rest of the orchestra could follow his lead.

As written music grew more complex, orchestras needed more direction than a keyboardist or violinist could provide. They needed someone to *orchestrate* the music. Conductors started appearing in France in the 18th century and emerged in earnest early in the 19th century. Still, there was no baton—rolled up paper was the tool of choice.

German composer, violinist, and conductor Louis Spohr claimed to have introduced the formal baton to the music world in a performance in 1820, but that simply might have been boastfulness. It is widely thought that he only used a baton in rehearsals.

It's possible that German composer, pianist, and conductor Felix Mendelssohn was the first to use an actual baton in a performance. According to *The Cambridge Companion to Conducting*, Mendelssohn used a baton in 1829 and again in 1832 with the Philharmonic Society of London. The next year, a baton was used regularly with the Philharmonic—and today, almost every conductor wields one.

Baton Wackiness

Even though the baton is a lot safer than the wooden staff, there have been some accidents along the way. For example, German conductor Daniel Turk's motions became so animated during a performance in 1810 that he hit a chandelier above his head and was showered with glass. What is it with these guys?

There was more baton craziness in 2006 and 2007. First, the conductor of the Harvard University band set a record by using a baton that was ten and a half or 12 and half feet long, depending on whom you listen to. The next year, the University of Pennsylvania band claimed to have bested that record with its 15-foot, nine-inch baton. There were no reports of a Lully moment on either occasion.

WHAT EXACTLY IS A DOUBLE REED?

Modern double reed instruments began to take shape during the Renaissance. Instrument makers experimented with medieval woodwind designs, coming up with various shapes before achieving the designs we see in modern orchestras. Double reed instruments have two thin pieces of wood (usually cane), called reeds, fitted closely together in the front of the mouthpiece. The reeds vibrate as air is blown past them. Double reed instruments date back thousands of years. The ancient cultures of the Middle East, Egypt, and Greece all had double reed instruments. Medieval Europe had the shawm and crumhorn. The oboe, bassoon, contrabassoon, and English horn are all modern descendants of this ancient instrument family.

The Oboe

The oboe is a thin, black tube with metal keys. It is shorter than a clarinet, and has a higher pitch and thinner sound. The oboe's unusual tone can create lively, happy-sounding music or slow melodies that sound sad and mysterious. The oboe is probably a descendant of the medieval shawm. Orchestras in France started using the oboe in the 1600s. It has had a place in Classical orchestras since the 1700s.

The Bassoon

The bassoon was invented during the seventeenth century, when many types of similar double reed instruments were used. Its design was gradually improved until it became a preferred lower-register woodwind in orchestras. The modern bassoon is usually made of maple wood. It has a great range: it can play powerful and heavy low notes or expressive, vocal-sounding high notes. Like the oboe, it can play in a wide variety of musical moods.

The Contrabassoon

At an octave below the bassoon, the contrabassoon (often simply referred to as the "contra") is frequently the lowest-sounding instrument in an orchestra. At its lowest, it can have the same rasping tone as a double bass. Strangely enough, its unusual tone is perfect for creating two very different moods: it can lend an ominous, spooky feeling to a song, or it can sound very comical. If the instrument were stretched out straight, it would be about 18 feet long. The contrabassoon is somewhat rare in orchestras.

The English Horn

The English horn is actually not a horn at all, but a close relative to the oboe. It is slightly bigger, and is capable of playing lower notes. It is known for a sound that can be haunting and melancholy or mellow and romantic. The rounded bell at the end of the instrument helps to shape the sound.

WHO WERE THE ROMANTIC COMPOSERS?

The musical era of Romanticism (roughly 1820–1900) is an important period in the development of classical music, spawning some of the greatest composers and connecting the European classical (1730–1820) and modernist periods.

Romanticism as it pertained to music in the 19th century did not simply refer to music that was soft, moody, and dreamy. The idea behind romanticism was that it strived to capture powerful emotional expression. Romantic composers explored the limits of the forms they inherited from the Classical period. Special attention was paid to how the forms could express emotions. They added new chords, better instruments, and expanded dynamics to increase the emotion in their music. They began to write music based on poems, stories, and paintings. They found inspiration in nature, the supernatural, exotic themes, and folklore. Romantic composers also paid attention to *tone color*, the special sound that makes an instrument unique. They used tone color to expand the emotional range of music. The music of this period may remind you of the music you hear during a movie. In fact, many film scores use the same techniques found in Romantic music. Audiences still respond to the expressiveness of Romantic compositions.

One important factor of the period was that talented, free-thinking composers were able to support themselves with their work. One cannot live on accolades alone, after all. Public concerts became a popular way for composers to survive while enjoying creative freedom—not having to suffer the whims of the ecclesiastical and imperial patronage long associated with classical music.

Ludwig van Beethoven (1770–1827)

Generally considered the first and most pivotal of the romantic era musicians, Beethoven is one of the most towering and influential composers of all time. At first he imitated great composers such as Haydn, but as his talent matured, he created daring and original pieces that changed the course of music. Two popular examples of his early romantic style are the Moonlight and Pathétique Sonatas. Beethoven ultimately lost his hearing, but proof of his genius lies in the fact that he continued to compose, conduct, and perform regardless. Beethoven was known as a very quarrelsome individual, but he is now believed to have suffered from bipolar disorder.

Hector Berlioz (1803–69)

A French romantic composer, Berlioz contributed greatly to the importance of the modern orchestra. He sometimes wrote music for a thousand musicians. His *Symphonie Fantastique* is considered a classic example of romantic-era composition—because of its hallucinatory, dreamlike overtones, some experts believe it was written under the influence of opium. Berlioz also provided the musical arrangement of Rouget de Lisle's "La Marseillaise," the French national anthem. Although extremely influential in symphonic composition, his genius was not acknowledged until the early 1960s.

Franz Liszt (1811–86)

This Hungarian composer is credited with inventing the symphonic poem. A close friend of Berlioz, Liszt was also instrumental in the popularity of his *Symphonie Fantastique*. Liszt may have been the Liberace of his time—not only an accomplished piano virtuoso, but a profound entertainer as well. His *Hungarian Rhapsodies* and Piano Sonata in B Minor have entered the realm of composition classics. Unfortunately, Liszt's fall down a flight of stairs led to a number of ailments and, quite possibly, his death.

Johannes Brahms (1833–97)

This German composer spent much of his life in Austria. He began his career at an early age, playing in dance halls to help support his family. Previously considered a bland imitator of Beethoven, he is now believed to have been a true innovator of rhythmic conception and a prime example of the late period of romanticism. Brahms is frequently labeled the most truly "classical" romantic composer. His *Hungarian Dances* are extremely popular, and his "Wiegenlied" is the world's most familiar lullaby, lulling children to sleep in practically every known language.

Frédéric Chopin (1810–49)

A Polish-born child prodigy, Chopin was already hailed as a genius when he settled in Paris at age 21. Considered by critics to be one of the world's greatest composers of piano music, he was also an accomplished concert performer. His stormy romantic relationship with French writer George Sand (whose real name was Aurore Dupin) has been the subject of several novels and motion pictures. It was this relationship that stimulated him to write some of his greatest works. Chopin's refined and complex waltzes are among the most popular piano recital pieces ever composed. Never a healthy man, he died of tuberculosis at age 39.

Peter Ilyich Tchaikovsky (1840–93)

Possibly the last of the romantic-era masters, this Russian composer was known for his brilliant orchestrations and strong melody lines. The popular song "Tonight We Love," recorded by Freddy Martin in 1941, was adapted from one of his most familiar works, the Piano Concerto No. 1 in B Flat Minor.

WHO WAS LIBERACE?

Like his singing counterpart Elvis Presley, Liberace entered the world with a stillborn twin. But Liberace, christened Wladziu Valentino Liberace and usually called "Lee" or "Walter," was born with part of the birth sac over his head. Throughout the ages, the birth sac (or caul) has been seen as a mystical portent of special talents or powers, and in this case, the old wives' tale got it right: few human beings have possessed Liberace's magical power to enthrall a crowd.

Born to Beguile

Born in 1919, in West Allis, Wisconsin, young Walter was a sickly boy. He spoke with an odd accent that he later compared to Lawrence Welk's, although it may have come from seven years of speech therapy. Nevertheless, he could joyously pound out piano tunes by the time he was three, and, at age seven, he won a scholarship to the Wisconsin School of Music.

As a young teenager, Liberace soloed with the Chicago Symphony, as he originally wanted to be a classical concert pianist. He also hammered the ivories in silent-movie houses in the Milwaukee area.

In 1939, he had a revelation after being asked to play a popular song, "Three Little Fishes," at the end of a classical concert in LaCrosse, Wisconsin. When the crowd went wild over the way he hammed up the song, he realized his destiny lay in entertaining the masses with humor and glitz.

By the early 1950s, Liberace was playing Carnegie Hall and Madison Square Garden. On May 26, 1954, he grossed a record $138,000 at the Garden. He was also a hit on TV with *The Liberace Show*. He received many awards—two Emmy awards, six gold albums, Entertainer of the Year, and two stars on the Hollywood Walk of Fame (one for music and one for television). He was over-the-top, and people loved him for it.

The Gatherer of Glitz

Liberace began wearing flashy clothing so he could easily be seen in huge auditoriums. He soon discovered that the glitzier he became, the more audiences loved him. His wardrobe progressed from a simple gold lamé jacket to such unparalleled items as a blue fox cape that cost $300,000 and trailed 16 feet behind him, a sequined red-white-and-blue drum major suit that substituted hot pants for trousers, a sparkly silver cape garnished with mounds of pink feathers, and a black mink cape lined with rhinestones. One of his most outrageous getups was a King Neptune costume that weighed 200 pounds.

Liberace loved to surround himself with luxurious symbols of his music. The best-known example was his piano-shape pool. He loaded his house with diamond- and crystal-studded candelabras and other objects—lamps, planters, bookends—fashioned in the shape of a baby grand. Today, much of his fabulous collection can be seen at the Liberace Museum in Las Vegas. The massive stash includes 18 pianos, such as the famed concert grand completely surfaced with tiny squares of mirror, and a Baldwin glittering with rhinestones.

Liberace's legendary wardrobe is there, too, along with his famous jewelry. He often wore five or six huge rings on each hand while performing, such as the behemoth adornment shaped like a candelabra, with diamond flames dancing over platinum candlesticks. Many of his baubles were shaped like pianos, including his wristwatch, which was studded with diamonds, rubies, sapphires, and emeralds. Even his automobiles were decorated Liberace-style: he had a Roadster slathered in Austrian rhinestones and a Rolls-Royce covered in mirror tiles.

The Liberace Museum also includes a re-created version of Liberace's lavish bedroom from his Palm Springs home. It features examples of his collection of exclusive Czech Moser crystal and a desk once owned by Russian Czar Nicholas II.

Nunsense?

Despite his great wealth (the *Guinness Book of World Records* once listed him as the highest-paid musician and pianist), Liberace was often prone to illness. In November 1963, he was near death from kidney failure caused by breathing toxic fumes from his costumes. He was calling relatives and friends to his hospital bed so he could say goodbye and give away his earthly goods, when he was suddenly and inexplicably cured. His explanation for the miracle was that a mysterious white-robed nun had come into his room and told him to pray to St. Anthony, patron saint of missing things and lost persons, then she touched his arm and left. Liberace never discovered who the nun was or where she came from, but he did recover.

Although raised Catholic, Liberace was very superstitious and was a great believer in numerology and fate. He insisted that his success was due to his favorite book, *The Magic of Believing*.

He Who Plays in Vegas, Stays in Vegas

Liberace eventually found a perfect venue for his talents in Las Vegas, where he bought a supper club just off the Strip called Carluccio's Tivoli Gardens. With its piano-shape bar and lavish decor, it was pure Liberace.

After Liberace's death from complications of AIDS on February 4, 1987, at least two psychics claimed that his spirit remained at the restaurant. Staff reported floating capes, doors mysteriously opening and closing, and unexplained electrical disturbances.

A magazine reporter, who accompanied investigators on a ghost hunt at Carluccio's almost two decades after "Mr. Showmanship's" death, wrote in a February 2005 article that the pair snapped a photo of a restaurant employee that revealed a ghostly form standing next to her. If ever there was a chance for one last photo op, Liberace would certainly find it very hard to resist showing his big smile for the camera.

HOW DID WE GET THE HAMMOND ORGAN?

Long before keyboard wizards such as Patrick Moraz, Keith Emerson, and Rick Wakeman made synthesizers and mellotrons essential gear in the rock 'n' roll tool kit, the Hammond organ was the straw that stirred the sound. As essential to the sounds that shaped the '60s as feedback and the fuzz box, the Hammond B-3 organ was capable of producing both soothing, liquid tones, and gritty, textured accompaniment. It provided a whirring cascade of effects that enlivened soul, jolted jazz, and revolutionized rock.

The Hammond organ as we know it was designed and developed by Laurens Hammond in 1933. A graduate of Cornell University, Hammond had invented a soundless electric clock in 1928. He used a similar technology to construct his revolutionary keyboard, adapting the electric motor used in the manufacture of his clocks into a tonewheel generator, which artificially re-created or synthesized the notes generated by a pipe organ.

By using drawbars to adjust volume and tone, Hammond was able to electronically simulate instruments such as the flute, oboe, clarinet, and recorder. Thaddeus Cahill, who created an instrument dubbed the *telharmonium* in 1898, first formulated the concept of the tonewheel generator. While it was dynamic in design, it was cumbersome in concept, weighing seven tons and costing $200,000 to produce. Not exactly the potentially portable keyboard that Hammond was able to perfect 30 years later.

The effectiveness of Hammond's electric keyboard was greatly enhanced by the invention of the Leslie tone cabinet, a system that uses a rotating speaker to amplify, adjust, and enhance the intricacies of the Hammond sound. Invented by Donald Leslie in 1937, it proved to be a perfect partner to complement Hammond's keyboard, although there was bitterness between the two men, who thus never established a business partnership. The Hammond B-3 was first manufactured in 1955. It remains a favorite among jazz musicians and rock groups.

1. What part of the bagpipe vibrates as air passes over it, creating the initial sound?
a. The string
b. The double reed
c. The single reed
d. The membrane

2. What is an alphorn?
a. A very long wooden horn associated with the mountain dwellers of Switzerland
b. A horn made from the curved horns of the Alpine ibex
c. A passage in classical music featuring only brass instruments
d. An extra valve on a brass instrument

3. Where did opera come from?
a. England
b. Egypt
c. Italy
d. Russia

4. Which pitch range is the lowest?
a. Baritone
b. Soprano
c. Mezzo-soprano
d. Alto

5. How many unique notes exist in a major scale?
a. 5
b. 7
c. 9
d. 16

6. What is the name for musical notation for guitar showing finger positions?
a. Tablas
b. Taboret
c. Clef tabs
d. Tablature

7. What do piano hammers strike to make a sound?
a. Strings
b. Hollow metal tubes
c. Hollow wooden tubes
d. Metal blocks

8. What Scott Joplin-penned ragtime song is now associated with ice cream trucks?
a. "The Ice Cream Truck"
b. "The Ice Cream Man"
c. "I'm Sweet on You"
d. "The Entertainer"

9. How many keys does a typical modern piano have?
a. 52
b. 100
c. 88
d. 54

10. The vibrating parts of the harmonica responsible for creating sounds are called:
a. Tonewheels
b. Resonators
c. Reeds
d. Needles

1.
b. The double reed

2.
a. A very long wooden horn associated with the mountain dwellers of Switzerland.

3.
c. Italy

4.
a. Baritone

5.
b. 7

6.
d. Tablature

7.
a. Strings

8.
d. "The Entertainer"

9.
c. 88

10.
c. Reeds

MILITARY MATTERS

THE RIGHT WAY, THE WRONG WAY, AND THE ARMY WAY

The military is baffling to a civilian. If a lieutenant ranks below a major, then shouldn't a lieutenant general rank below a major general? And why do they need all those stars, bars, and jargon in the first place? If you don't salute a colonel because your hands are full, do you get thrown in the brig? What's a brig? Even if you have a handle on the jargon, there are acronyms to contend with. Most of us know an MRE is a Meal Ready to Eat, but how about NFG and BFO? (Non-Functioning Gear and Blinding Flash of the Obvious—but there are variations.) And how about SNAFU's pal, TARFU? (We'll let you work that one out).

DO ALL COUNTRIES HAVE MILITARY FORCES?

Who wants to know? You looking to start some trouble? Okay, we give: there are 21 countries that do not have formal forces. Some have components of a military, such as a Coast Guard, while others have relatively large police forces that may dabble in a little national security on the side.

Most countries that do not have sustainable defensive military forces have a "you scratch my back, and I'll get my back scratched" deal with other nations. France, for instance, is responsible for Monaco, and it shares the responsibility of defending Andorra with Spain. Australia and New Zealand would help out Kiribati if needed. New Zealand must consider all requests for military aid by Samoa in accordance with the most sweetly named treaty ever, the Treaty of Friendship (1962). And of course, Italy would probably have something to say to anyone who tried to mess with the Rome-based Vatican City, although Italy and the Vatican do not have a defense treaty because it would violate the Vatican's neutrality.

Beginning in 1951, Iceland had a deal with the United States that had U.S. forces stationed there until 2006, when they withdrew. While the U.S. no longer has a physical presence there, Iceland and the United States have signed a Joint Understanding to continue a "bilateral defense relationship." Since Iceland does have a Coast Guard, there are some things Iceland can share with us. In addition to Iceland, the U.S. is responsible for defending the Marshall Islands, the Federated States of Micronesia, and Palau, since they are associated states—free entities with political ties to the United States.

Dominica, Grenada, Saint Lucia, and Saint Vincent and the Grenadines do not have official military forces, but they are all protected under the Regional Security System (RSS). The RSS is an agreement among many Caribbean countries to protect one another. Haiti, Costa Rica, and a few other small countries don't have militaries, but they do have extensive police forces, some of which have paramilitary units. Haiti's military, while disbanded, still exists on paper in its Constitution.

So, while some countries aren't exactly armed to the teeth, it would still require more than a few drunken friends and some slingshots to take them over.

HOW MANY COUNTRIES HAVE A NEUTRALIST POLICY?

Bent on world domination? To an aspiring dictator, neutral countries can look like the low-hanging fruit on the tree of global conquest. They lack offensive military capabilities and they have wishy-washy foreign policies—in other words, they are there for the taking. Or so it would seem. In fact, this whole "neutral" thing is a lot more complicated than it looks.

First of all, there's a difference between being "neutral" and "neutralist." A neutralist country is one that has a policy of nonalignment: when it seems like the whole world is picking sides in an extended conflict, a neutralist country will try to stay out of it. The neutralist movement dates back to the Cold War, when some countries refused to affiliate with either the Soviet bloc or the Western bloc of nations. India is one of the largest countries that had a neutralist policy—it tried to (ahem) curry favor with the USSR and the USA alike. But a neutralist policy doesn't mean a country must avoid aggression. Neutralist countries have gone to war with each other, like Iran and Iraq did in the early 1980s.

So how many neutralist countries are there? Quite a few. So many that they have their own international organization, the Non-Aligned Movement (NAM), which represents most of the countries in South America, Africa, and the Middle East. And though the NAM has been called a relic of the Cold War, it's still alive and kicking.

Now, a "neutral" country is something else entirely. Neutrality is a condition that is recognized by the international laws and treaties that govern warfare. According to these agreements, when a war breaks out, disinterested countries can declare themselves neutral. This means that they have certain rights— the warring nations can't enter their territories, for example— as well as the fundamental responsibility to remain neutral by treating the warring nations impartially. Any country can potentially remain neutral during any war, as long as it can maintain that impartiality.

But this idea of limited neutrality doesn't really get to the heart of our question. We're looking for perpetually neutral countries—the Swedens and the Switzerlands of the world. Switzerland, as you may recall, has had guaranteed neutrality since the Congress of Vienna settled Napoleon's hash in 1815, and the Swedes have been neutral since about that time as well. But although Sweden stayed out of the great wars of the twentieth century, its current neutrality is debatable since it's a member of the European Union (EU) and, as such, has a stake in the EU's non-neutral foreign policy.

That leaves the Swiss. But before you start drawing up your marching orders against the soft underbelly of Switzerland, you should get familiar with the phrase "armed neutrality." This means that the Swiss aren't going to roll over for you—they've got a defensive army, or more accurately, a sort of citizen militia. Switzerland also has one of the highest gun-ownership rates in the world. So beware, aspiring dictators: this world-domination thing isn't as easy as it looks.

WHY DO SOLDIERS SALUTE?

The military depends on deeply ingrained rituals in order to accomplish just about everything it does. The horrors of combat can become even worse if military personnel fail to follow orders to the tee or waver in their service and mission. Even in less-intense situations, such as the close quarters of everyday military life, maintaining a strictly enforced sense of decorum is critical.

So members of the armed forces of the United States salute as a way of regularly reinforcing their respect for the chain of command, for the country, and for each other. This simple gesture is one of many matters of formal courtesy woven into the fabric of the military.

Militaries of other countries follow similar practices, though the details may vary. They're all honoring a custom that goes back so far that no one is certain how it got started. Nevertheless, two explanations are likely: many historians believe that civilians in ancient Rome raised their right hands when approaching military officers or other public officials. This was originally a way of showing that the civilian wasn't preparing to stab the official with a dagger (assassinations were something of a problem in ancient Rome).

Other historians believe that medieval knights in full armor raised their visors when approaching each other to signal that they meant no harm. This became a sign of respect, and it evolved into touching the brim of the hat or removing the hat, and, finally, into a version of the modern salute.

Today, each branch of the United States military has specific guidelines for when saluting is appropriate. As a general rule, members of the armed forces salute all officers in any branch of the U.S. military or any allied military whenever they are in uniform and outdoors. The lower-ranking person is supposed to be the first to salute, and then the higher-ranking officer returns the gesture.

In addition, members of the military are expected to salute the president, who is also commander in chief of the armed forces, and any recipient of the Medal of Honor. Saluting is mandatory when raising or lowering the flag; during the national anthem and when other ceremonial music is played; when rendering reports; and during particular ceremonies, such as funerals and changes of command.

Because guidelines for each branch get a little complicated, saluting when it's not absolutely required is generally acceptable. Failing to salute when it's expected, on the other hand, is considered deeply disrespectful.

WHY DO U.S. SOLDIERS WEAR A BACKWARD AMERICAN FLAG ON THEIR SHOULDERS?

It's a symbol of good old-fashioned bravery. The flag patch on the U.S. Army uniform is the modern-day incarnation of a time-honored tradition: carrying flags into battle. But instead of schlepping a big flag on a pole onto the field, as a standard bearer would have done in the Revolutionary War or Civil War, modern soldiers simply wear flags on their uniforms.

To keep true to the tradition, there's an imaginary pole that leads the way. Army regulation states that the flag should "be worn so that to observers, it looks as if the flag is flying against a breeze." On the right shoulder, this means that the stars—the "union," in flag-speak—are on the right. The same goes for flags that are on the right sides of vehicles and aircraft. If the flag was pointed the other way, with the union on the left side, it would look as if the soldier was carrying the flag away from the battle. And that's not how the Army rolls.

If you think about the patch this way, the flag isn't really backward. After all, you wouldn't say that a flag on a pole is backward if you see it from the side and the stars are on the right. But it rightly seems backward, because the flag code dictates that whenever the flag is against a wall, as in artwork, the union should be to the left. At any rate, don't try this at home, unless you want the flag-code police banging on your door. Leave the "backward" flags to the professionals.

1. In the army, which of the following ranks the highest?
a. Lieutenant colonel
b. Lieutenant general
c. First lieutenant
d. Captain

2. The U.S. Air Force began existence as:
a. The Army Air Corps
b. The Navy Air Corps
c. The National Air Defense
d. The Department of Aeronautical Research

3. Which of the following is the largest U.S. army unit?
a. Squad
b. Brigade
c. Platoon
d. Battalion

4. In what year did the last American cavalry charge take place?
a. 1898
b. 1902
c. 1942
d. 1878

5. When was the U.S. Marine Corps founded?
a. 1775
b. 1776
c. 1812
d. 1824

6. Armored tanks made their first appearance in this war.
a. The American Civil War
b. World War I
c. World War II
d. The Spanish Civil War

7. Which country has the largest standing army in the world?
a. India
b. Russia
c. United States
d. China

8. What does the D in D-Day stand for?
a. Destruction
b. It doesn't stand for anything.
c. Delivery
d. Destiny

9. Which of the following presidents held the highest military rank?
a. Dwight D. Eisenhower
b. James Garfield
c. Thomas Jefferson
d. Andrew Jackson

10. How many countries possess nuclear weapons?
a. 2
b. 5
c. 9
d. 15

1.
b. Lieutenant general

2.
a. The Army Air Corps

3.
b. Brigade

4.
c. 1942

5.
a. 1775

6.
b. World War I

7.
d. China

8.
b. It doesn't stand for anything.

9.
a. Dwight D. Eisenhower

10.
c. 9